Introduction

o you realize that you're already in space? u're on the planet Earth, which rotates on its is once every 24 hours. Earth, in turn, orbits e Sun. Earth is one of nine planets in our solar stem.

The Sun is just one of billions of stars in our laxy, the Milky Way. The Milky Way, in turn, is e of billions of galaxies in the universe.

This book is about astronomy—the study of ace. Chapter 1 introduces the universe and w our view of it has changed over time.

apter 2 explores our corner of the universe— e Earth, the Sun, and the Moon. (These words e capitalized to distinguish them from other ns, moons, and planets in the universe.)

Chapter 3 looks at the other inner planets of r solar system: Mercury, Venus, and Mars. apter 4 ventures outward to Jupiter, Saturn, anus, Neptune, and Pluto. Chapter 5 focuses features like asteroids, comets, and meteors.

Chapter 6 steps beyond our solar system to plore the stars. Chapter 7 examines the past, esent, and future of space exploration. Chapter sks if we are alone in this vast universe.

Some parts of the book talk about what scientists believe or think. That's because we still don't know everything there is to know about space. We're constantly discovering new things.

Even without wearing a spacesuit, you can explore ideas about space here on Earth. Enjoy the hands-on activities throughout this book. Always use caution and common sense, and ask an adult to help you when needed.

Astronomical Numbers feature neat math facts about space. Far-Out Facts tell interesting items about astronomy and space exploration.

You'll also find profiles of Space Cadets. These men and women from different backgrounds have all contributed to our understanding of space. Their courage and dedication show there's a place in space science for everyone.

So, read on and enjoy *The Everything Kids' Space Book*. Perhaps one day you'll not only be in space, but go up in space too. In any case, the more we learn about space, the more we understand about ourselves and our universe.

—Kathiann M. Kowalski

Acknowledgments

my thanks to the following people who have helped me understand more about space and the ace program: Guion Bluford, Martin Glicksman, Mary Hardin, David Meisel, Wendell Mendell, rc Millis, Kathleen Needham, Alain Poirier, Lori Rachul, Donna Shirley, Dennis Stocker, thleen Sullivan, James Van Laak, Michael Wargo, William Wilcox, and Eric Williams. Thanks o to my editor, Cheryl Kimball. Last, but by no means least, thank you to my husband, Michael issner, and to our children, Chris, Laura, and Bethany, for their understanding support and pful comments.

THE
EVERYTHING KIDS' SPACE BOOK

All about rockets, moon landings, Mars, and more plus space activities you can do at home!

Kathiann M. Kowalski

Adams Media Corporation
Holbrook, Massachusetts

This book is dedicated to my parents,
Edward and Julianna Kowalski.

An Everything® Series Book.
Everything® is a registered trademark of Adams Media Corporation.

Published by Adams Media Corporation
260 Center Street, Holbrook, MA 02343
www.adamsmedia.com

ISBN: 1-58062-395-6

Printed in the United States of America.

J I H G F E D C B A

Library of Congress Cataloging-in-Publication Data available from the publisher.

Cover illustrations by Joseph Sherman.
Interior illustrations by Kurt Dobler and Kathie Kelleher.
Puzzles by Beth Blair.
Series editor: Cheryl Kimball

Puzzle Power Software by Centron Software Technologies, Inc. was used to create puzzle grids.

This book is available at quantity discounts for bulk purchases.
For information, call 1-800-872-5627.

Table of Contents

CHAPTER ONE

WELCOME TO THE UNIVERSE!

WORDS to KNOW

orbit: travel around another body in space in a regular path. [OR-bit]

matter: the "stuff" that makes up the physical universe; generally, anything that has weight and takes up space.

In the Night Sky

Look up in the sky on a clear, dark night. What do you see?

First, there are stars. Away from city lights, you may see up to 3,000 stars. Look closely to spot constellations. These star groups seem to move through the sky during the night and throughout the year. Ancient people imagined that constellations, like connect-the-dots pictures, showed story heroes and animals.

Stars are so far away that their light takes years to reach us. Some are "only" a few light years away. The light from other stars has traveled thousands and millions of years. Telescopes let us see even farther back in time for billions of years.

Then there are planets. Called "wanderers" by ancient people, they appear as small dots. We spot planets as they reflect light from our Sun.

Like Earth, planets go around, or **orbit**, the Sun. Some you can see with the naked eye. Planets farther away become visible only with a telescope.

The Moon looms large in the night sky. It is the closest celestial body to Earth. The Moon changes appearance as it orbits the Earth. At some parts of the month, it is a full, glowing circle. Other times it's a crescent sliver. Other planets' moons orbit them too.

The night sky offers other sights as well. Asteroids too small to be planets orbit the Sun. Meteors streak across the sky. Comets sometimes hover like glowing balls with brilliant tails.

Finally, there's the black background of space itself. Most of space is a vast vacuum. That means it has basically nothing in it. But occasional bits of stuff, called **matter**, do float through space. There are atoms of hydrogen and other elements. There are even tinier bits, like the charged particles from the solar

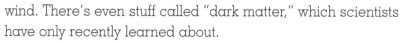
wind. There's even stuff called "dark matter," which scientists have only recently learned about.

Space is all this, and more. Space is truly *everything* that's out there.

Ancient Observers

Since ancient times, people have marveled at space. They saw the Sun rise and set at different points each day. At night, the Moon, stars, and planets likewise moved across the sky in an arc.

Stonehenge in southern England was one ancient observatory. Stonehenge means "hanging stones." Its oldest part is a circular ditch 320 feet (97 meters) across. It dates back to 2600 to 3000 B.C. Inside the circle made by the ditch stand stone pillars and crossbeams weighing up to 45 tons (20 tonnes). Their construction dates from 1800 to 2100 B.C. Lines made by certain stones marked where the Sun rose or set at key times, like the solstices. The winter solstice, around December 21 in the Northern Hemisphere, has the least amount of daylight. The summer solstice, with the most daylight, falls around June 21 north of the equator.

The ancient Maya built the Caracol observatory at Chichén Itzá. It's on the Yucatán Peninsula in Mexico. Among other things, the Caracol had windows that showed the Sun's and Moon's setting on the spring equinox, which falls about March 21. Equinoxes are days when the amount of sunlight and darkness are equal. Knowing when the equinoxes and solstices occurred helped ancient people plan farming and other activities.

The Maya could predict solar and lunar eclipses, as well as the orbit of Venus. They also developed three calendars. A 365-day

FUN FACT

Light Pollution

The closer you are to a city, the harder it is to see the stars. Some states, like New Mexico and Texas, have now passed laws restricting new light pollution. Ontario, Canada, has set up an area as a dark sky preserve.

Elsewhere, you'll have to try to plan around light pollution. Nap early in the evening. Then you can watch the sky after mall and grocery store lights go out. Also find areas that are less likely to be lit up. A beach in winter or a large park can get almost as dark as a remote rural area. Check the place's rules in advance to be sure you're allowed in after dark. Of course, never go alone, always go with a trusted adult.

Last, but not least, check the weather report before heading out. Even dark skies won't show stars with clouds overhead.

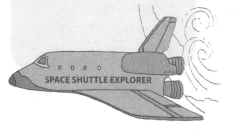
SPACE SHUTTLE EXPLORER

Astronomical Numbers

What's a Light-Year?

Space scientists use light years to talk about how far away things are. A **light-year** (abbreviated ly in science experiments and math equations) is the distance light travels in one year.

In just one second, a beam of light travels about 186,000 miles, or 300,000 kilometers. In a year, that adds up to 5.9 trillion miles, or 9.4 trillion kilometers. A trillion is 1, followed by 12 zeroes.

When you see a star, you're really looking back in time. For example, Regulus, a star in the constellation Leo, is 85 light-years away. The light you see as that star has traveled 85 years to reach Earth.

Here are the approximate distances of some stars from Earth:

Star Name	Light-Years from Earth
Proxima Centauri (closest after Sun)	4
Sirius (in Canis Major)	9
Altair (in the Summer Triangle)	16
Vega (in Lyra)	26
Pollux (in Gemini)	35
Denebola (in Leo)	39
Betelgeuse (in Orion)	520
Antares (in Scorpio)	520
Rigel (in Orion)	900
Deneb (in Cygnus)	1,600

solar calendar governed activities like planting corn. A 260-day calendar with 13 "months" of 20 days each served religious purposes.

The Maya also used a Long Count. For that calendar, 400 years of 360 days each made a *baktun*. Every 13 *baktuns*, the Maya believed the world would end and be recreated.

Other civilizations—including ancient Babylonians, Egyptians, Chinese, and Greeks—watched the skies too. The more people learned about astronomy, the better they could plan their lives. Astronomy was also important in the religions of different cultures.

WORDS to KNOW

light-year: the distance light travels in one year; about 5.9 trillion miles or 9.4 trillion kilometers.

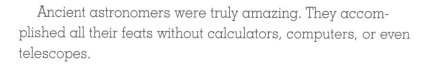

Ancient astronomers were truly amazing. They accomplished all their feats without calculators, computers, or even telescopes.

Changing Views of the Universe

Viewed from Earth, the Sun moves across the sky from east to west each day. At night, the Moon, planets, and stars likewise seem to rise and set. No wonder most ancient cultures believed that Earth must be at the center of the universe.

During the second century A.D., the Greek astronomer Ptolemy formed complex theories to "prove" this view. People accepted his theories for more than 1,000 years.

Then Nicolaus Copernicus (1473–1543) of Poland had a new idea. Copernicus was an official of the Catholic Church and a physician. He spent many nights studying the stars and planets. Copernicus did not think that Earth was the center of the universe. Rather, he believed, Earth and the other planets revolved around the Sun. Copernicus wrote his ideas down in a booklet called *Little Commentary*. The booklet formed the basis for a longer book called *Concerning the Revolutions of the Heavenly Spheres*. Copernicus received the first printed copy of the book just before he died in 1543.

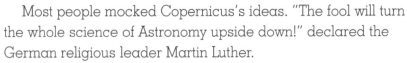

WORDS to KNOW

galaxy: a huge group of stars, gas, dust, and other matter orbiting their common center of mass. [GAL-ax-ee]

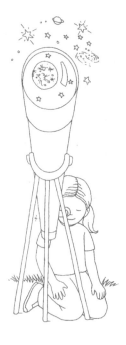

Most people mocked Copernicus's ideas. "The fool will turn the whole science of Astronomy upside down!" declared the German religious leader Martin Luther.

Gradually, however, people thought about Copernicus's ideas. In defiance of orders from the Catholic Church, the Italian monk and philosopher Giordano Bruno (1548–1600) wrote and taught about Copernicus's theory. Using the newly invented telescope, Johannes Kepler (1571–1630) of Germany and Galileo Galilei (1564–1642) of Italy also decided Copernicus had been right. Copernicus's views made even more sense when Sir Isaac Newton (1643–1727) of England explained planets' orbits with gravity and motion.

Over time, even religious authorities accepted that Earth isn't the center of the universe. It took a long time, but Copernicus's theories were proved correct.

Still, our view of the universe was less than complete. Until early in the 20th century, it seemed that our Milky Way galaxy was all there was. A **galaxy** is a gigantic collection of stars and their associated planet systems.

In the 1920s, American astronomer Edwin Hubble (1889–1953) showed that other galaxies existed beyond our own Milky Way. The Milky Way is huge—about 75,000 light years across. Today we know it's just one of billions of galaxies in our universe.

The Telescope: Our Eye on the Sky

In 1608, Hans Lippershey (c.1570–1619) of the Netherlands held one optical lens in front of another. He noticed that distant objects seemed bigger and closer. By mounting the lenses in a tube, Lippershey built one of the first telescopes.

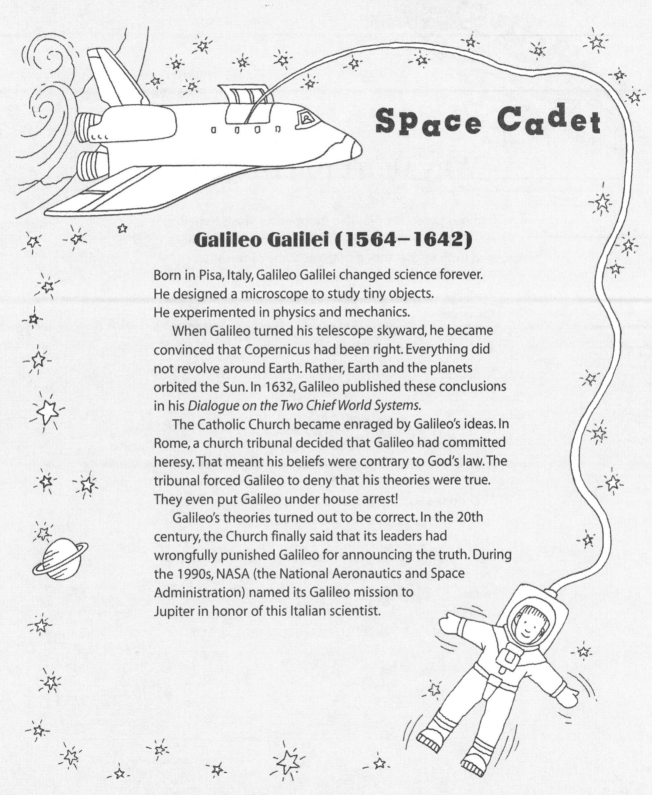

Space Cadet

Galileo Galilei (1564–1642)

Born in Pisa, Italy, Galileo Galilei changed science forever. He designed a microscope to study tiny objects. He experimented in physics and mechanics.

When Galileo turned his telescope skyward, he became convinced that Copernicus had been right. Everything did not revolve around Earth. Rather, Earth and the planets orbited the Sun. In 1632, Galileo published these conclusions in his *Dialogue on the Two Chief World Systems.*

The Catholic Church became enraged by Galileo's ideas. In Rome, a church tribunal decided that Galileo had committed heresy. That meant his beliefs were contrary to God's law. The tribunal forced Galileo to deny that his theories were true. They even put Galileo under house arrest!

Galileo's theories turned out to be correct. In the 20th century, the Church finally said that its leaders had wrongfully punished Galileo for announcing the truth. During the 1990s, NASA (the National Aeronautics and Space Administration) named its Galileo mission to Jupiter in honor of this Italian scientist.

Note: Ask an adult to help you with this one!

Why Don't You Drop By?

In a famous experiment, Galileo dropped two balls from Italy's Tower of Pisa. One ball was heavy. The other was light. Galileo wanted to show that they'd both fall at the same rate.

Try your own version of Galileo's experiment.

You need:
- A place outside where the ground is soft
- A portable ladder or small platform such as a sturdy chair
- Metal 5-pound (2.25-kilogram) and 1-pound (1/2-kilogram) weights

1. Ask an adult to help you climb *carefully* onto the ladder or platform. Let the adult hand you the two weights.
2. Hold the weights level with each other. Be sure the ground beneath is soft and free from objects that might get hurt.
3. Drop the two weights at exactly the same time. They should hit the ground simultaneously.

Earth's gravity makes objects fall at the rate of 32 feet per second per second. Sometimes this is written as 32 ft/sec^2 (9.8 m/sec^2). At the end of the first second, an item falls at 32 feet (9.8 meters) per second. At the end of the next second, the rate is 64 feet (19.6 meters) per second. And so on.

Soon after, Italian scientist Galileo Galilei improved the telescope. Turning it toward the heavens, Galileo saw craters and mountains on the Moon. He saw Jupiter and discovered four of its moons. He saw millions of stars in the Milky Way.

Johannes Kepler also studied the planets with a telescope. He discovered that planets' orbits are oval shaped, or elliptical, rather than round.

In 1668, Sir Isaac Newton improved the telescope by putting mirrors in it. Telescopes with mirrors are called reflector telescopes. They are still used today.

Over the next centuries, astronomers made startling discoveries with their telescopes. They saw the "new" planets Uranus, Neptune, and Pluto. They spied asteroids and comets.

Astronomers also observed details on known objects in the sky. In 1877, for example, Italian scientist Giovanni Schiaparelli (1835–1910) noted *canali*, or channels, on Mars.

As time passed, astronomers used larger and more powerful lenses and mirrors for their telescopes. Some modern reflecting telescopes are huge. Atop Mauna Kea in Hawaii, 36 hexagonal mirrors measuring 6 feet (1.8 meters) across join together to make each telescope's 11-yard (10-meter) primary mirrors. Other huge telescopes scan the skies at the McDonald Observatory in Texas, the Whipple Observatory and Kitt Peak in Arizona, Palomar Observatory in California, Zelenchukskaya in Russia, and elsewhere. At Cerro Paranal in Chile, the Very Large Telescope (VLT) will combine images from four 9-yard (8.2-meter) telescopes.

Many modern observatory telescopes are hooked up to cameras and computers. People can view images from other locations and analyze data faster than ever before.

Take a closer Look

A telescope makes distant objects look closer and more clear. See if you can find where each close-up picture is located in the big space picture. Write the correct coordinates (letter and number) on the lines provided. Careful: Some pictures might be upside-down or sideways!

1._____ 2._____ 3._____ 4._____ 5._____ 6._____ 7._____ 8._____

Nonetheless, Earth based telescopes still get a less-than-perfect view of the universe. Just as water in a lake blurs the sky above, the atmosphere blurs our view of space.

To see space without that distortion, NASA launched the Hubble Space Telescope (HST) in 1990. In 1993, the shuttle *Endeavor's* crew made in-space adjustments. Following those repairs, HST has shown us star nurseries and galaxies farther away than anyone had ever seen. It has literally given science a new view of the universe.

Beyond Visible Light

Hold a prism up to the sunlight, and look at the rainbow image it projects. The prism separates white light into its different wavelengths. We see these wavelengths as the colors red, orange, yellow, green, blue, indigo, and violet. After a rainfall, water droplets can also act as prisms. We see a rainbow as the longer red and yellow wavelengths curve over the shorter green, blue and violet wavelengths.

Light also has other wavelengths, both below and above the visible spectrum. Things that don't appear in one type of light sometimes show up in others. Special telescopes "see" these wavelengths.

Around 1936, American Grote Reber invented the first radio telescope. Using his 31-foot (10-meter) metal dish, Reber collected radio waves from all over the Milky Way, especially its center. Radio waves are similar to the wavelengths used for broadcasting radio and television.

Everything Kids'

http://www.

Astronomy Picture of the Day

antwrp.gsfc.nasa.gov/apod/astropix.html
What more can we say? See a new image each day.

New York Times on the Web—
Exploring the Solar System

www.nytimes.com/library/national/science/solar-main.html
Get statistics and news stories about our solar system.

Puerto Rico's 1,000-foot (300-meter) Arecibo radio telescope is huge. Another huge radio telescope system is the Very Large Array (VLA) in New Mexico. It combines radio wave images from 27 radio telescopes spread out in a huge Y.

Just below visible light is infrared light. Even before the light from new stars can be seen with regular telescopes, infrared telescopes show the mounting heat in the stars' masses. NASA has an Infrared Telescope Facility in Hawaii at Mauna Kea. Other infrared telescopes orbit Earth, such as the Infrared Space Observatory, which was launched in 1995.

Just above the visible spectrum is ultraviolet light (UV). These wavelengths can give you a sunburn and eventually cause cancer. But in space, UV light gives astronomers another view of the universe.

X-rays and gamma rays have even shorter wavelengths than ultraviolet light. These wavelengths don't penetrate Earth's atmosphere easily, so scientists observe them with orbiting telescopes. The Advanced X-Ray Astrophysics Facility and Chandra X-Ray Observatory are examples of X-ray telescopes.

The Compton Gamma Ray Observatory detects gamma ray bursts. Gamma ray bursts are unpredictable intense flashes of tremendous energy that can happen anywhere in the sky. Scientists think they come from billions of light-years away, but they're still not sure what causes these powerful energy bursts.

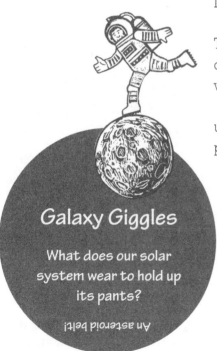

Galaxy Giggles

What does our solar system wear to hold up its pants?

An asteroid belt!

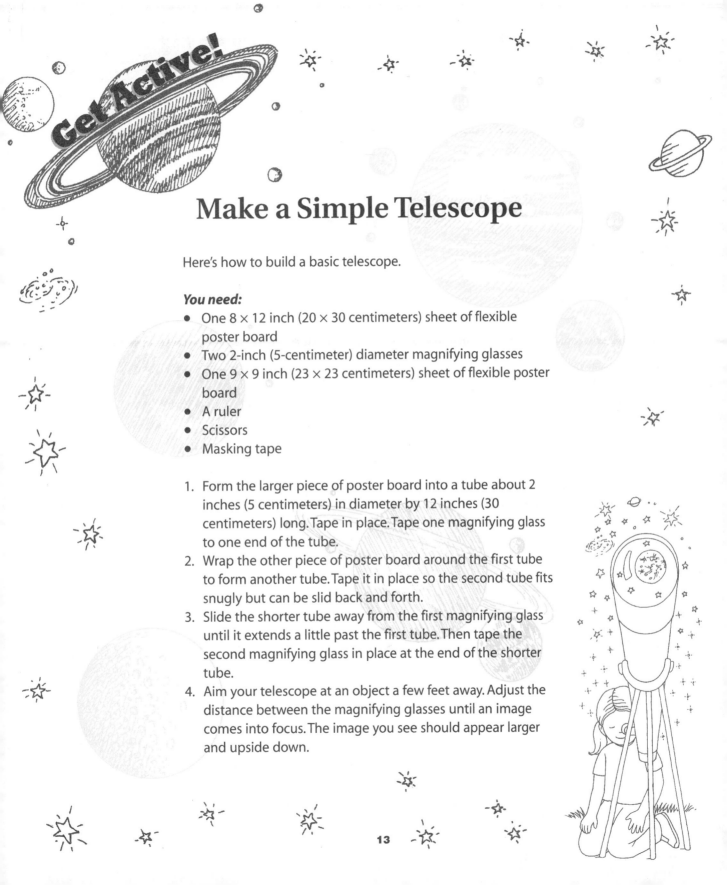

Get Active!

Make a Simple Telescope

Here's how to build a basic telescope.

You need:
- One 8 × 12 inch (20 × 30 centimeters) sheet of flexible poster board
- Two 2-inch (5-centimeter) diameter magnifying glasses
- One 9 × 9 inch (23 × 23 centimeters) sheet of flexible poster board
- A ruler
- Scissors
- Masking tape

1. Form the larger piece of poster board into a tube about 2 inches (5 centimeters) in diameter by 12 inches (30 centimeters) long. Tape in place. Tape one magnifying glass to one end of the tube.
2. Wrap the other piece of poster board around the first tube to form another tube. Tape it in place so the second tube fits snugly but can be slid back and forth.
3. Slide the shorter tube away from the first magnifying glass until it extends a little past the first tube. Then tape the second magnifying glass in place at the end of the shorter tube.
4. Aim your telescope at an object a few feet away. Adjust the distance between the magnifying glasses until an image comes into focus. The image you see should appear larger and upside down.

Stephen Hawking

At England's Cambridge University, Stephen Hawking studies theoretical physics. His ideas about the origin of the universe, black holes, gravity, and other complex issues are at the "cutting edge" of science. But he is able to explain complex ideas to nonscientists. His book, *A Brief History of Time*, became the best-selling science book in history.

Soon after his 21st birthday, Stephen learned he had ALS, or amyotrophic lateral sclerosis. Also known as Lou Gehrig's disease, ALS slowly paralyzes most voluntary muscles. Few patients live more than five years.

ALS put Stephen in a wheelchair. He needs round-the-clock nursing care. He speaks only with a computerized speech synthesizer.

But Stephen's science career has soared despite ALS. He has met the challenges of the disease and advanced our understanding about space and the universe.

SPACE SHUTTLE EXPLORER

Our view of the night sky improves as scientists use different kinds of telescopes. That gives us a clearer understanding of our universe.

The Big Bang

We know our universe is "out there." But where did it come from?

The big bang theory is the leading scientific theory on how the universe developed. It says that back at the beginning of the universe, all energy and matter were packed together in an incredibly tiny spot. Something then happened to make that tiny spot explode. When it exploded, the tiny spot burst into what we know as space. As a result of that big bang, the theory says, we exist in an ever expanding universe.

Observations support the big bang theory. For example, distant galaxies are moving away from Earth. The farther away a galaxy is, the faster it moves away from Earth. That makes sense if the universe is still expanding after an ancient explosion from a single spot.

The big bang theory explains a lot, but what caused the big bang? Scientists have different theories about what happened, but no one can prove them. Some people believe that God created and designed the universe. Other people think the matter just happened to be there.

Science may only be able to go so far. Mysteries and unanswered questions still remain.

All Blown Up

See why things move apart in an expanding universe.

You need:
- A light colored helium-quality balloon
- Red and black nonsmearing ballpoint pens
- Measuring tape

1. Draw spirals around the surface of the balloon with the black pen. These spirals represent galaxies in the universe. Using a red pen, draw two spirals larger than the others. Let the ink dry.
2. Measure the distance between the red spirals. Blow the balloon up. Then measure the distance between the red spirals again. As the balloon expands, the red spirals get farther apart.

Of course, not everything moves away from other things. Earth, for example, orbits the Sun because of gravity. Nonetheless, galaxies' movement away from each other suggests that the universe is still expanding after an ancient event.

Astronomical Numbers

How old Is the Universe?

In the early 1990s, NASA sponsored a team of 27 scientists from different places to study data from the Hubble Space Telescope. Eight years later, in 1999, the team announced that they had determined that the universe is between 12 and 15 billion years old.

First, they estimated how fast the universe seems to be expanding. That rate is called the Hubble constant. The team's best guess is 44 miles (70 kilometers) per second, per megaparsec. A megaparsec is 3.3 million light-years.

The scientists allowed a margin of error of 10 percent. In other words, the actual number could be 10 percent greater or smaller than their best guess. Then the scientists used math to estimate the universe's age.

We already knew the universe was old. Now we know that it's *really* old!

What Shape Is the Universe?

This is a great question, but scientists don't yet know the answer. Space seems to extend forever in all directions. Each direction also seems to expand at the same rate as other directions. Yet first appearances aren't always correct.

Land, for example, appears to extend flat in every direction. In reality, however, Earth is round. Go far enough in any direction, and you'll wind up back where you started.

Space may well extend in all directions like an ever expanding sugar cube. Or, it may have a much flatter shape, like a cracker or cookie.

Space may also extend in all directions in what mathematicians call a hyperbolic shape. Like a potato chip or saddle, it may curve up at some places and down at others.

Leaving Home

Traveling in outer space can be a tricky business. Can you get the space ship from Earth to Mars?
Avoid the asteroids, satellites, black holes and solar flares!

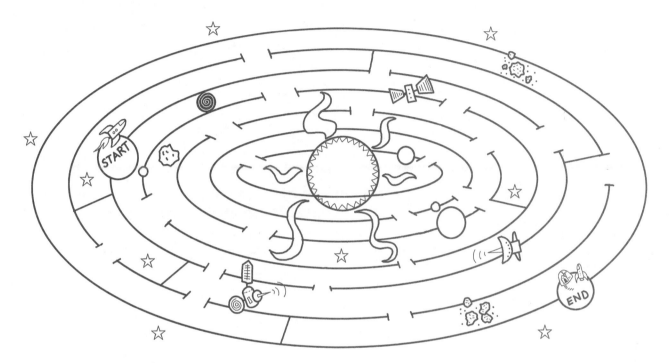

Does space fold back on itself? Suppose that space was shaped like a doughnut. If so, starting in one place may—after billions of light years—bring you back where you started. Additional holes or loops may even provide "shortcuts" through the universe. Scientists and storywriters call these theoretical shortcuts "wormholes."

Another possible form may be a four-dimensional soccer ball. In theory, going out-ward from one of its 60 faces may bring you back on the opposite side. The possibilities go on and on.

Why does shape matter? Shape and curves affect how large things appear. In regular three-dimensional geometry, objects of the same size seem smaller as they get far-ther away.

Angles and relative size may change, however, if the universe differs from what we

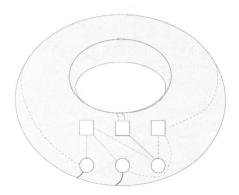

assume. Think of how funhouse mirrors can confuse you.

Shape also affects what's possible. Draw three squares in a row on a piece of paper. Then draw three circles in a row underneath them. No matter what you do, you can never draw one line from each square to each circle without crossing at least one line.

Suppose, however, that you use a toothpick to draw the circles and squares on a doughnut. Now the hole in the middle lets you connect each circle to each square without crossing lines. (Be sure to clean up the crumbs after you eat the doughnut!)

Most observations so far suggest the universe has a flattened shape or a hyperbolic shape. Who knows how our understanding of the universe will finally shape up?

CHAPTER TWO

THE SUN, EARTH, AND THE MOON

Sun Worshipers

The ancient Egyptians believed the Sun was the falcon-headed god Re, who was reborn each day at sunrise. Ancient people in India worshiped the Sun as their god Surya. In Central America, the Aztecs offered human sacrifices to their sun god Tonatiuh

The Blue Moon

A blue moon doesn't look blue. One definition used for about 50 years says a blue moon is the second full moon in a calendar month. In 1999, scientists said a blue moon is really the fourth full moon in a season.

Either way, blue moons occur rarely. If someone promises you something "once in a blue moon," don't hold your breath waiting.

TTLE EXPLORER

The Sun: Earth's Super Star

The Sun is just an average-size star. Because we depend on the Sun for life, though, it's a super star to us.

The Sun provides energy for all living things on Earth. Green plants and certain bacteria make food in a process called photosynthesis. They combine water and carbon dioxide in the presence of sunlight. The result is a simple sugar that cells use for energy.

Other living things can't make their own food. Still, they get energy indirectly from sunlight. They eat things that made their food with photosynthesis. Or, they eat other organisms that ate plants.

Deep under the earth, scientists recently found bacteria that make food from water and gases in the rock. Similar single-cell creatures thrive near deep sea vents. Even those organisms indirectly rely on the Sun. If the Sun hadn't formed, Earth wouldn't be here now, and neither would any living thing.

During the year, Earth's distance from the Sun averages 93 million miles (149 million kilometers). Light traveling at 186,000 miles (300,000 kilometers) per second takes eight minutes to reach us from the Sun.

Compared to Earth, the Sun is huge. The diameter at its equator measures 865,000 miles (1.4 million kilometers) across. If the Sun were a giant ball, it could hold more than 1.3 million Earths.

One Huge Hot Spot

The Sun is our solar system's hot spot. Through a process called **nuclear fusion**, it combines hydrogen atoms to make helium. In the process, the Sun radiates heat and light for our planet.

The Sun shines with 380 billion trillion watts of power. That's 380, followed by 21 zeroes. That's brighter than all the light bulbs on Earth put together.

The corona is the outside edge of the Sun's atmosphere. It's visible only during a total eclipse. Large explosions, called prominences, sometimes shoot out from the corona.

The chromosphere is the next layer down. Hot jets of gas, called flares, shoot up here.

Next comes the photosphere. Huge cells, called granules, change in shape and size as heat rises from the Sun's center. Temperatures at the bottom of the photosphere reach 12,400°F (6,900°C).

Beneath the sun's photosphere lies the convective zone. In this region, convection makes hot fluids rise and cool fluids sink. Thus, most heat in this zone circulates. Beneath that is the radiative zone where heat flows outward. And below that is the Sun's dense core. The core is where nuclear fusion occurs. Temperatures there reach more than 28 million°F (15.7 million°C).

How long will the Sun keep shining? The Sun is about 5 billion years old already. Its hydrogen fuel will last another 6.4 billion years.

More than Sunshine

The Sun provides light and heat to Earth and parts of our **solar system**. But the Sun affects Earth in other ways too.

Magnetic disturbances in the photosphere cause sunspots and flares. Sunspots look like dark splotches. They are somewhat cooler than the rest of the Sun.

WORDS to KNOW

nuclear fusion: the process by which stars produce tremendous amounts of energy by joining atoms of one element to form another element. [NOO-clee-ar FYOO-shun]

solar system: the Sun and its associated planets, asteroids, comets, and so on. [SO-lur SIS-tem]

Solar Poetry

Can you finish this poem to our sun?

Twinkle, twinkle, little _____,

I used to wonder what you _____.

(Now I know EVERYTHING!)

When hydrogen meets _____,

And fuse to create _____,

You, in the process, shine so _____,

You twinkle, twinkle, day and _____.

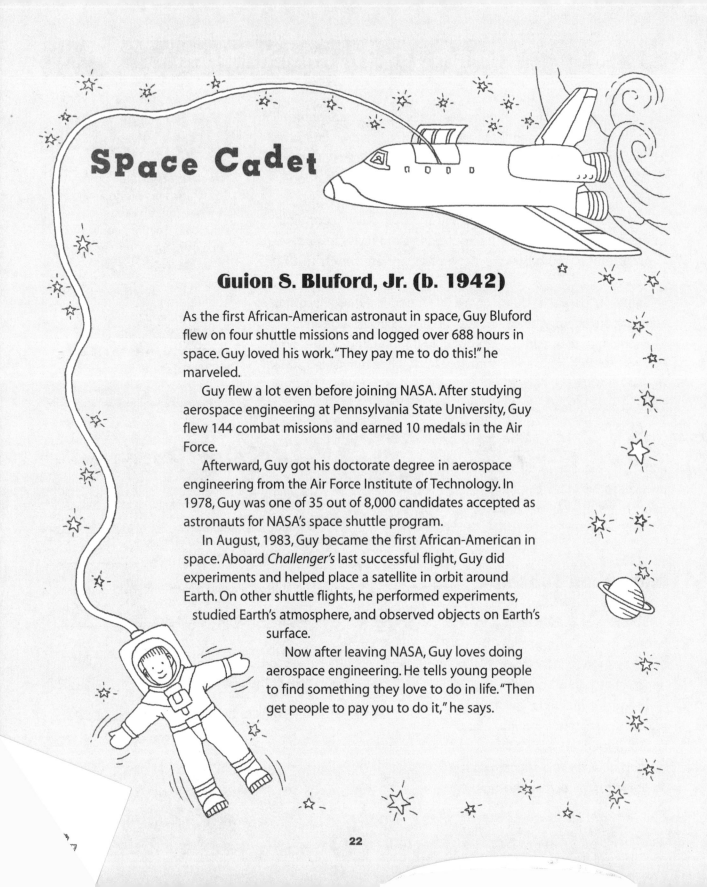

Space Cadet

Guion S. Bluford, Jr. (b. 1942)

As the first African-American astronaut in space, Guy Bluford flew on four shuttle missions and logged over 688 hours in space. Guy loved his work. "They pay me to do this!" he marveled.

Guy flew a lot even before joining NASA. After studying aerospace engineering at Pennsylvania State University, Guy flew 144 combat missions and earned 10 medals in the Air Force.

Afterward, Guy got his doctorate degree in aerospace engineering from the Air Force Institute of Technology. In 1978, Guy was one of 35 out of 8,000 candidates accepted as astronauts for NASA's space shuttle program.

In August, 1983, Guy became the first African-American in space. Aboard *Challenger's* last successful flight, Guy did experiments and helped place a satellite in orbit around Earth. On other shuttle flights, he performed experiments, studied Earth's atmosphere, and observed objects on Earth's surface.

Now after leaving NASA, Guy loves doing aerospace engineering. He tells young people to find something they love to do in life. "Then get people to pay you to do it," he says.

Solar flares shoot up hot jets of gas. That sends charged particles called protons and electrons into the solar system. Hydrogen protons have a positive charge. Electrons have a negative charge. Movement of these charged particles through space is called the solar wind.

Sunspots and flares peak about every 11 years. The most recent peaks came in 2000 and 1989. The next peak will fall around 2011. As solar activity varies, Earth feels the effects.

In 1989, a solar storm disrupted transformers in Quebec, Canada. Six million people lost power for nine hours. The solar wind can also interrupt radio transmissions and satellite communications. Over 600 satellites in orbit around Earth control communications, air-traffic control, computer relays, and many other activities. Interruption of those services could be disastrous.

Too little solar activity causes problems too. Toward the end of the 17th century, astronomers saw few sunspots. That period also brought unusually harsh winters on Earth and generally cooler weather. The lack of sunspots may have caused the abnormal weather.

Planet Earth

Planet Earth gives us a place to live, air to breathe, food to eat, and lots of other great stuff. What does Earth's status as a planet mean?

For one thing, Earth revolves around the Sun. It takes about 365 ¼ days, or one year, for Earth to complete its orbit.

Planet status also means that Earth is old. Our planet formed about 4.6 billion years ago. Dust and gas swirled around the young Sun. Over millions of years, some of the dust and gas came together to form Earth. (Some of the rest formed

FUN FACT

Differential Rotation

The Sun isn't solid, so different parts rotate at different rates around its axis—a phenomenon called differential rotation.

From the surface down through the convective zone, regions near the equator take about 25 days to complete a rotation. Areas closer to the Sun's poles, however, move more slowly and take about 35 days to finish their rotation. Deeper inside the Sun, the radiative zone and core seem to rotate all at the same rate, as if they were a solid body.

Lunar Calendars

Not everyone uses a solar calendar of 365 days. The Chinese calendar, for example, is a lunar calendar. Its months are based on the Moon's orbits around Earth. That's why the Chinese New Year and other holidays fall on different dates in our solar calendar each year.

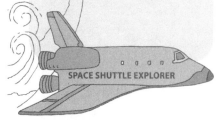

SPACE SHUTTLE EXPLORER

Astronomical Numbers

Hot Stuff

Temperature scales measure how much heat something has. In the United States, most people use degrees Fahrenheit, shown as °F. Scientists and most other countries measure temperature in degrees Celsius, written °C. On the Celsius scale, 0°C is the freezing point of water. The boiling point of water at sea level equals 100°C.

Scientists also sometimes use the Kelvin scale, or °K. It uses Celsius units, but its zero is absolute zero. Absolute zero is the point where all molecular motion stops. It equals –273°C. So, to get from °C to °K, subtract 273.

Converting °F to °C and back gets trickier. To get from °F to °C, subtract 32 and multiply by 5/9. So, 70°F = (70-32) × 5/9, which equals 21°C. To go from °C to °F, reverse the process. Multiply °C by 9/5 and add 32. Thus, 10°C = (10 × 9/5) + 32, which equals 50°F.

How do Celsius temperatures feel in the real world? Remember this popular rhyme:

30 is hot,
20 is nice,
10 is cool, and
Zero is ice.

other planets, while some was "blown away" into space.)

The liquid-iron core at our planet's center is extremely hot—about 8,500°F (4,700°C). Pressure and radioactivity account for much of the heat. Some heat probably remains from our planet's formation billions of years ago.

Surrounding the core is a plastic-like mantle with lots of iron and magnesium. Above that is a granite and basalt crust. In many areas the crust is covered by still more rock, including sandstone, shale, limestone, and clays.

Earth is a dynamic planet. Large areas of land, called tectonic plates, "float" on the mantle. The moving plates cause different geological effects. At some edges, lava spews out in volcanic eruptions.

At other edges, plates push together and upward to make majestic mountains. The Himalayas and Appalachians formed this way, for example.

A Bit of a Stretch

The more distant a galaxy is from Earth, the faster it moves away from us. Sound like a stretch? See for yourself.

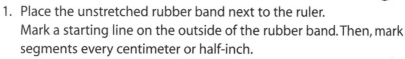

You need:
- A rubber band
- A ruler
- A watch with a second hand
- A pen

1. Place the unstretched rubber band next to the ruler.
   Mark a starting line on the outside of the rubber band. Then, mark segments every centimeter or half-inch.
2. Hold the starting line against the edge of your ruler. Note where the segment lines lie. Keep a firm grip on this end of the ruler.
3. Gently stretch the rubber band for 5 seconds. If you can reach the end of the ruler, loop the rubber band over the edge. Otherwise, hold it in place.
4. How far did your first centimeter or half-inch mark move in 5 seconds?
5. Where did the mark farthest from your starting point end up? Since both spots moved for the same amount of time, the spot that moved farther traveled faster.

Scientists don't have a giant ruler in the sky. Instead, they measure the speed at which things move away with a phenomenon called the Doppler effect.

The Doppler effect causes light from objects moving away to shift to a lower, redder frequency. Scientists say those objects are red-shifted. Using sensitive instruments, scientists measure the Doppler effect in light from distant galaxies. The Doppler effect shows that more distant galaxies are indeed moving away faster.

FUN FACT

The Northern Lights

Brilliantly colored lights often streak across the night sky in Arctic areas. Sometimes they flash. Other times, they shimmer and dance.

These lights are the aurora borealis, or northern lights. Similar colors light up the sky near the South Pole. They're the aurora australis, or southern lights.

Our Sun causes these beautiful skyworks. Charged particles in the solar wind react with Earth's magnetic field near the poles. That excites atoms in Earth's upper atmosphere 65 to 250 miles (100 to 400 kilometers) above the ground. The excited atoms glow, and we see the northern or southern lights.

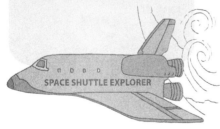

SPACE SHUTTLE EXPLORER

Plates slipping against each other can cause earthquakes. Plate activity makes California and the Pacific Northwest especially vulnerable to earthquakes.

Other plates meet at deep trenches where parts of the crust seem to go back down into the mantle. Because of tectonic plate movement, the oldest rocks found on Earth are less than half a billion years old.

Days, Seasons, and Years

Earth **rotates** on its axis once every 24 hours. When our part of Earth rotates toward the Sun, we have day. When it rotates away from the Sun, we have night.

Time zones account for the fact that the Sun rises and sets at different times in different places. A sphere has 360 degrees, so each hour brings another 15 degrees of the Earth's surface into or out of sunlight.

Earth orbits the Sun every 365 ¼ days. Because its axis tilts about 23 degrees, we have seasons. To see why, ask a friend to shine a flashlight at a globe. Then move the globe in a circle around the flashlight. Notice which parts of the globe are lit most brightly.

Areas near the equator get strong direct light year-round. They also enjoy warm, balmy weather year-round. For areas farther north or south, things are different.

During June, the Northern Hemisphere is tilted most toward the Sun. The Sun's rays shine most directly there as summer begins. It's also when days are longest.

WORDS to KNOW

rotate: to spin on an axis. [RO-tate]

moon: a body in space that orbits a planet.

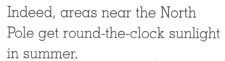
Indeed, areas near the North Pole get round-the-clock sunlight in summer.

At the same time, the Southern Hemisphere points away from the Sun. The light striking there is more spread out. Temperatures are cooler, days are shorter, and winter begins. Areas near the South Pole get 24 hours of darkness each day.

Six months later, the situation is reversed. In December, the Southern Hemisphere gets direct sunlight, and its summer starts. Places near the South Pole now have 24 hours of sunlight. Meanwhile, it's winter in the Northern Hemisphere.

The Moon

Reflecting the Sun's light, the **Moon** is the brightest object in the night sky. Watch it throughout the month to see its different phases.

The new moon phase comes at the start of the lunar month. Because the Moon lies between Earth and the Sun, we don't see the Moon.

Astronomical Numbers

How Earth Measures Up

Our planet's diameter is 7,928 miles (12,685 kilometers) at the equator. From pole to pole, it's only 7,901 miles (12,642 kilometers). Earth's spinning causes the slight bulge at the equator. Technically, the shape is an oblate ellipsoid, but it's fine to just say Earth is round.

How Many Days in a Year?

Calendars of 365 days and leap years were used since ancient times. But they didn't quite match Earth's movements around the Sun. In 1582, Pope Gregory XIII decided to fix things. Here's how the Gregorian calendar now works.

Most of the time, an Earth year is 365 days long.

However, since the revolution takes about an extra ¼ day, years divisible by 4 are leap years. Leap years have 366 days.

But if a year ends in two zeroes, it's not a leap year, *unless* the year is divisible by 400.

Confused? Just check your calendar.

Earth's Magnetic Field

Why do compasses point north? The reason is Earth's magnetic field.

Scientists believe the field results from convection currents in Earth's core. The movements produce an electromagnetic current. That, in turn, sets up the magnetic field.

Interestingly, the direction of Earth's magnetic field can change over time. If you had a compass a million years ago, it would have pointed south, rather than north.

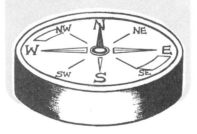

Traveling around 2,290 miles (3,660 kilometers) per hour, the Moon makes its 1.5-million-mile (2.4-million-kilometer) orbit around Earth. Soon we see the crescent moon, and then the quarter moon. After about two weeks, the Moon shines full.

As the Moon continues its orbit, it darkens again. Within a week we see the third-quarter moon. Then we see just a sliver. Finally, the new moon again starts another lunar month.

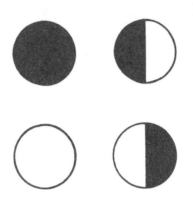

Orbiting about 235,000 miles (376,000 kilometers) from Earth's surface, it takes the Moon 27 days, 7 hours, 43 minutes, and 12 seconds to complete one full orbit. Earth moves too, though, so the period from one full moon to another is about 29.5 days.

As it orbits Earth, the Moon rotates. Its rotation is exactly as long as its orbit—a phenomenon called synchronous rotation. Thus, the same side of the Moon always faces Earth.

Aim strong binoculars or a telescope at the Moon, and you can see impact craters. **Craters** formed when comets, asteroids, or other material crashed into the Moon. Most craters are surrounded by a mountainous rim. That material settled after being thrown up on impact.

Force from a crash can make craters much larger than the objects that initially fell there. Crater Clavius is about 144 miles (232 kilometers) across. Its area could reach from New York to Philadelphia, Pennsylvania.

WORDS to KNOW

crater: round indentation made by the impact of an object from space on a planet or moon. [CRAY-tur]

Making Faces

Astronomers have always seen the shapes of people and animals in the sky. Here's a picture of the full moon. Connect the numbered craters first, and then connect the craters marked with letters. When you are finished, use the "Phases of The Moon Decoder" to find the name of this familiar person-in-the-sky!

Write the letters of the secret name in the boxes provided.

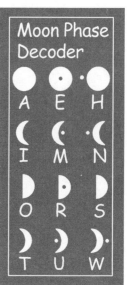

Moon Phase Decoder

A	E	H
I	M	N
O	R	S
T	U	W

Get Active!

Create Craters

See how impacts cause craters. To minimize cleanup, wear old clothes and do this activity outside. A clear day with almost no wind works best.

You need:
- A plastic food container, about 8 × 10 inches (20 × 25 centimeters)
- All-purpose flour
- A colored powdered drink mix
- Small objects of varying size and weight, like marbles, rocks, and golf balls
- A ruler
- Pencil and paper

1. Fill the container with flour until it's about 2 inches (5 centimeters) deep. Sprinkle a couple of teaspoons of drink mix lightly on top. This is your simulated Moon surface.
2. Drop the different objects onto your Moon surface from a height of 1 foot (30 centimeters). Gently lift each object off the surface. Write down the height and depth of the crater made by each object.
3. Repeat step 2, but this time drop each object from a height of 1 yard (90 centimeters).

Eighty to 150 meteoroids weighing from 4 ounces (100 grams) to 1 ton (1,000 kilograms) strike the Moon each year. Without an atmosphere to protect it, the Moon's surface bears the brunt of these repeated impacts.

Even without a telescope, you can see dark spots on the Moon. But that's not a man in the Moon you see. Rather, they're the Moon's maria. Maria means "seas" in Latin, but there's no water in these seas. The dark color of these plains comes from lava that seeped onto the surface. Scientists aren't sure why, but most maria are on the side facing Earth.

Mare Imbrium, also known as the Sea of Rains, or Showers, is the largest mare. It measures about 700 miles (1,100 kilometers) across—the distance from Cleveland, Ohio to Miami, Florida. Other maria include the Mare Nubium (Sea of Clouds), Mare Serenitatis (Sea of Serenity), and Mare Nectaris (Sea of Nectar). Humans first walked on the Moon at the Mare Tranquillitatis, the Sea of Tranquility.

The other 85 percent of the Moon's surface is called terrae, meaning land, or lunar highlands. Compared to the maria, the lunar highlands have many more craters. This makes sense if lava in the maria covered over some craters. Thus, maria probably formed after the lunar highlands.

The Moon measures 2,173 miles (3,476 kilometers) across at its equator. Because its size and mass are much smaller than Earth's, its gravity pull is less too. If you weighed 100 pounds (45 kilograms) on Earth, you'd weigh only about 17 pounds (8 kilograms) on the Moon.

Still, the Moon's gravity affects Earth. It causes tides, or twice daily swellings of Earth's oceans. The highest tides, called spring tides, come when the Sun, Earth, and Moon line up with each other. Spring tides occur during the new-moon and the full-moon phases. Lower tides occur when the Moon, Earth, and Sun form a 90-degree angle. These are called neap tides and occur at the quarter-moon phases.

FUN FACT

A New Day

By agreement, a new date starts at the International Date Line, which runs from north to south around 180 degrees longitude. When it's midnight Monday in New Zealand, it's only midnight Sunday just east of the International Date Line. Thus, travelers going west "lose" a day. Travelers headed east "gain" a day.

High Noon

North of the tropics, the midday Sun appears to the south. South of the tropics, it's to the north.

Right on the equator, the midday Sun shines directly overhead on the spring and fall equinoxes (about March 21 and September 21). For six months after the spring equinox, the midday Sun appears to the north. The other six months, it's to the south.

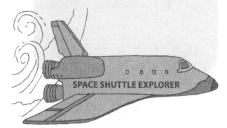

SPACE SHUTTLE EXPLORER

FUN FACT

Need Directions?

Global positioning systems use information from satellites to determine exactly where someone is on the planet. Then computers can use stored data about different locations to give people driving directions. Hikers, boaters, and mountain climbers also rely on global positioning systems.

Project EarthKAM

Want to photograph Earth from space? Using remote controls, EarthKAM lets students aim a camera aboard the space shuttle or International Space Station. EarthKAM Missions Operation Center processes the images at the University of California at San Diego. Then it posts the digital images on the Internet.

To learn how your class can participate, or to see photos other kids have taken, go to *www.earthkam.ucsd.edu*.

SPACE SHUTTLE EXPLORER

No Air and No Cheese

The Moon has no atmosphere. That means no air for people to breathe. It also means no air to carry sound. When astronauts visited the Moon from 1969 to 1972, they used radios in their spacesuits to communicate with each other.

On Earth, our atmosphere scatters sunlight. As a result, our sky looks blue. With no atmosphere, the Moon's sky looks black.

No atmosphere also means no blowing winds. Footsteps from NASA astronauts will stay on the lunar surface for eons.

No atmosphere also means no liquid water. Liquid water needs air pressure to keep it from boiling away.

The Moon *may* have ice. The 1994 *Clementine* mission and the 1998 *Lunar Prospector* mission suggest ice may exist at the Moon's poles. This would make a space station or even a business on the Moon much more practical. NASA has not yet confirmed the finding, however.

What about the rest of the Moon? An old saying held that the Moon was made of Swiss cheese. In reality, the Moon has an iron-rich core. Iron also makes up a lot of the surface, along with titanium, silicon, potassium, magnesium, calcium, and aluminum. Hydrogen and helium are present as well, including helium-3, an isotope that may one day provide fuel for nuclear fusion.

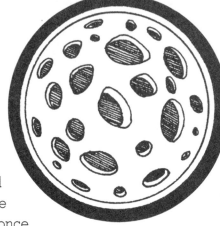

The Moon also has KREEP. KREEP is potassium (K), rare Earth elements (REE) like uranium and thorium, and phosphorus (P). KREEP may be what's left of the magma that once covered the Moon.

Where Did the Moon Come From?

Scientists aren't certain how the Moon formed. The most likely possibility is the collisional ejection theory. Here's how it goes.

Some giant object—maybe one as big as Mars—probably crashed into Earth shortly after our planet formed. The impact from such a collision 4.5 billion years ago would have shot debris into space. Gravity could then have pulled the debris together to form the Moon.

Astronomical Numbers

Lots of Rocks

Apollo astronauts brought 2,200 rock samples back to Earth from the Moon. The rocks weighed 842 pounds (382 kilograms). Unmanned Soviet spacecraft carried back another 2/3 pound (300 grams) of rocks. The moon rocks formed between 3 and 4.5 billion years ago.

Eclipses

If everything lines up just right, we see a solar or lunar **eclipse**. In a solar eclipse, the new moon blocks the Sun's light from reaching Earth. A total eclipse blocks all the Sun's light and briefly plunges the land into darkness. Flowers close up and bugs chirp just as if night had fallen. Even the wind changes.

A partial eclipse blocks only some of the Sun's light. Although it stays light out, the Moon's dark shadow covers part of the Sun's disk.

Then there's the annular eclipse. Like a giant Cheerio, the Moon's shadow is surrounded by a ring of sunlight.

Only certain parts of the world can see any given solar eclipse. An August 1999 total eclipse, for example, could be seen only from parts of the Atlantic Ocean, Europe, and southern Asia. Viewers who weren't too far away from the eclipse's path may have seen a partial eclipse. People in North

eclipse: the blocking of light from one object in space by another. In a *solar eclipse*, the Moon keeps all or part of the Sun's light from reaching parts of Earth. In a *lunar eclipse*, Earth blocks the Sun's light from reaching the Moon. [ee-CLIPS]

Artemis Society

www.asi.org
Is doing business on the Moon too out-of-this-world? The Artemis Society thinks it just might be possible.

EarthKAM

www.earthkam.ucsd.edu
EarthKAM lets middle school classes take real photos of Earth from space. See how your class can sign up, and view images taken by other kids.

and South America didn't see that eclipse.

If you can witness any solar eclipse, be careful. Even a fraction of the Sun's light could damage your eyes or cause blindness. To watch an eclipse, prick a pinhole in a piece of cardboard, and let the Sun's image shine through that onto another piece of cardboard. Or check with a local museum or astronomy group to see if they have filtered viewing opportunities.

Lunar eclipses, in contrast, can generally be seen with the naked eye. Of course, the sky must be clear and dark.

During a lunar eclipse, Earth's shadow keeps sunlight from shining directly on the Moon. Instead of disappearing, however, the shadowed Moon gets a reddish glow. The glow reflects long red lightwaves that filtered through Earth's atmosphere and scattered toward the Moon.

Why don't we get eclipses with every new moon or full moon? The Moon orbits Earth on a slightly different plane, or level, than Earth orbits the Sun. Usually, the new moon or full moon falls slightly above or below the plane of Earth's orbit, so light shines through.

CHAPTER THREE

THE INNER PLANETS:

MERCURY, VENUS, AND MARS

Mercury: Hot, Hot Days and Cold, Cold Nights

In Greek myths, Mercury was a winged messenger. In our solar system, Mercury is the closest **planet** to the Sun. Orbiting the Sun every 88 days, Mercury fits the image of a swift traveler.

Mercury is only 3,030 miles (4,880 kilometers) in diameter. About 50 percent bigger than our Moon, Mercury is the second smallest planet.

During Mercury's days, temperatures soar to 662°F (350°C). At night, temperatures dip to –274°F (–170°C).

Why such a big difference? Mercury has very little atmosphere. Scientists have detected atoms of sodium, helium, potassium, hydrogen, oxygen, and argon. But the atoms are so far apart that they barely bump into each other. Thus, no gas "blanket" holds the heat when the Sun sets.

Mercury's days are also quite different from Earth's. The planet rotates once every 59 Earth days. That's two-thirds as long as Mercury's 88-day orbit of the Sun. In other words, Mercury completes three rotations for every two of its years.

Mercury has no life as we know it. The temperatures are too extreme for any organisms like those on Earth.

A Cratered Planet

In 1974 and 1975, the *Mariner 10* spacecraft sent close-up pictures of Mercury's surface. Its huge craters look like parts of our Moon.

The Caloris Basin is Mercury's largest known

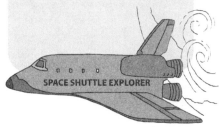

SPACE SHUTTLE EXPLORER

FUN FACT

Why Would Anyone Sit Under Newspaper?

People often remember the order of the planets with the sentence: "*My Very Excellent Mother Just Sat Under NewsPaper.*" The first letters of each word, plus the "P" in "newspaper," stand for Mercury, Venus, Earth, Mars, Jupiter, Saturn, Uranus, Neptune, and Pluto.

The silly sentence places the planets in their usual order moving away from the Sun.

WORDS to KNOW

planet: a spherical, nonshining body that orbits a star. Planets generally are larger than asteroids, although a few asteroids are larger than Pluto. [PLAN-et]

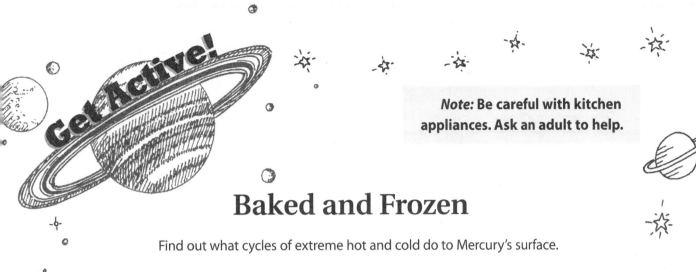

Baked and Frozen

Find out what cycles of extreme hot and cold do to Mercury's surface.

You need:
- A cookie sheet
- Aluminum foil
- 1 tube refrigerated cookie dough, cut up into cookies
- Potholders
- A spatula

1. Line one corner of the cookie sheet with a 4-inch (10-centimeter) square of aluminum foil. Place the pieces of dough on the cookie sheet so that one cookie will bake on the foil and the rest will bake on the cookie sheet. Bake the dough according to directions. Be sure to use potholders to lift the cookie sheet into and out of the oven.
2. After baking, use the spatula to remove the cookies that baked right on the sheet. Share these with family or friends. Keep the remaining cookie on the foil as you slide it off the cookie sheet.
3. When it's cool enough to handle, put the foil with the cookie in the freezer for 30 minutes. Wash and dry the cookie sheet.
4. Place the foil and cookie back on the clean cookie sheet. Bake the cookie again for 8 minutes at 325°F (163°C).
5. Repeat steps 3 and 4.

How does the surface of your cookie change with each round of baking and freezing? Mercury's surface endures even more extremes of hot and cold as the planet slowly rotates.

crater. It measures over 800 miles (1,300 kilometers) across. That's the distance from Milwaukee, Wisconsin, to Atlanta, Georgia.

Mercury's surface also shows many cracks, or fractures. Mercury's molten core may have expanded billions of years ago. That could have caused cracks on the surface. When the core cooled, the planet probably shrank a little. That could have caused more cracks. Constant cycles of hot and cold would add even more cracks.

Scientists believe that Mercury's core has lots of iron. The core seems to cover about 75 percent of Mercury's radius. In contrast, the planet's crust and mantle are comparatively thin. Did an ancient asteroid hit Mercury and smash the mantle and crust material away? Like most of Mercury's history, the answer remains a mystery.

Radar images from the 1990s show bright spots near Mercury's North Pole. Could the spots be water ice? Surface temperatures get very hot during the day. However, some craters near the pole might be shadowed all the time.

Mercury in Transit

Observing Mercury from Earth is a challenge. The Sun's brightness usually outshines the small planet. When Mercury is visible, it appears either right before sunrise or right after sundown.

On rare occasions, Mercury's path in the sky crosses the Sun. This phenomenon is a transit.

As always, you should never look directly at the Sun. To see a transit, scientists use special cameras and viewers. Then they see Mercury's small spot travel slowly across the Sun's disk. A transit in November 1999 was visible in much of North and South America.

Venus: The Cloudy Planet

As Earth's closest neighbor among the planets, Venus's average distance from the Sun is 68 million miles (108 million kilometers). Look for it as a bright "morning star" in the east before sunrise. Or scan the western sky just after sunset to see it as an "evening star."

Measuring 7,565 miles (12,104 kilometers) across at its equator, Venus is almost as big as Earth. However, we could not survive on Venus.

Venus gets even hotter than Mercury. The entire planet is shrouded in dense, thick clouds. Like a giant greenhouse, the clouds absorb sunlight. Hot infrared rays cannot reflect back to space, so surface temperatures reach 900°F (482°C). That's hot enough to melt lead!

If we didn't melt, Venus's atmosphere would poison us. It's 95 percent carbon dioxide. Nitrogen, argon, and sulfur dioxide make up most of the rest of the atmosphere. There's also sulfuric acid, hydrochloric acid, and hydrofluoric acid.

Venus has almost no water vapor. What "rain" it has falls as burning drops of sulfuric acid. Venus is so hot, however, that the drops evaporate before hitting the ground.

If we didn't melt or get poisoned, Venus's atmosphere would crush us. Air pressure at Earth's surface is 15 pounds per square inch, and our air is 1,000 times less dense than water. Venus's atmosphere is 90 times denser than Earth's.

The Surface of Venus

The United States and the former Soviet Union successfully landed spacecraft on Venus. Before the planet's heat and

FUN FACT

Global Warming Isn't Only on Venus

As "greenhouse gases" in Earth's atmosphere increase, fewer infrared rays can reflect back into space. By the year 2100, our planet's temperature could increase up to 6°F (3.5°C).

Earth will be nowhere near as hot as Venus. Yet just a few extra degrees could cause disaster. Melting even a small bit of Earth's polar ice could cause awful floods. And typhoons and hurricanes could become more common and more severe.

Fortunately, you can help. To save gasoline, walk sometimes or share rides with friends. Save energy at home by turning off unnecessary lights and appliances. Recycle wastes to reduce demands for raw materials and support programs to preserve rain forests whose plants absorb lots of carbon dioxide.

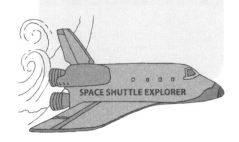

SPACE SHUTTLE EXPLORER

atmospheric pressure destroyed them, they sent photos and valuable information back to Earth.

Venus is a rocky world. Sunlight filtered through Venus's clouds bathed the planet in an orange glow. The rocks seem to be made of basalt, a material like that found on our ocean floors.

In the 1990s, NASA's *Magellan* spacecraft began mapping Venus. Using radar, it bounced radio energy pulses off the planet's surface. The results let NASA create maps and computerized three-dimensional images.

About two-thirds of Venus is low, rolling plains. Highland "continents" make up about another quarter of the surface. Aphrodite Terra is one of these continents. Ishtar Terra, another highland area, is about as large as Australia. The Maxwell Montes range near the edge of Ishtar Terra towers 7 miles (11 kilometers) high.

The rest of the surface is covered with volcanic areas. These volcanoes aren't active now. However, Maat Mons, the largest volcano, may recently have brought molten lava out from inside the planet. Volcanoes on Venus often have steep "pancake domes" formed from lava.

Remember that Earth's surface moves in large areas called tectonic plates. Venus isn't like that. Instead, its surface seems to have moved up and down. Scientists still aren't sure why or how that happened.

Venus probably formed when Earth and other planets did about 4.6 billion years ago. But Venus's 900 impact craters are only 300 to 500 million years old, which makes them much younger than those on our Moon. Was the planet resurfaced in the last half billion years? If so, scientists would like to know how.

Astronomical Numbers

A Year and a Day

Venus is the only planet where a day lasts longer than a year. Venus orbits the Sun in just under 225 Earth days, but a rotation on its axis takes 243 Earth days.

Mars: The Red Planet

Why is Mars called the red planet? Iron gives the planet's surface a reddish brown appearance. The red becomes even more distinct when we view the planet against the blackness of space. In fact, the reddish color was even the reason behind the naming of this planet. Mars was named for the bloody Roman god of war.

Mars measures 4,248 miles (6,796 kilometers) across at the equator. With less mass than Earth, Mars's surface gravity is also much less. If you weighed 100 pounds on Earth, you'd weigh only about 38 pounds on Mars.

Mars is a chilly world. Its average surface temperature is –82°F (–63°C). A day on Mars lasts 37 minutes longer than one of our days here on Earth. But Mars's average distance from the sun is about 142 million miles (228 million kilometers). Thus,

Solar System Sentence

Can you think of a new silly sentence to help remember the names and the order of the planets in our solar system?

M _____
V _____
E _____
M _____
J _____
S _____
U _____
N _____
P _____

Note: Do this activity with an adult.

The Greenhouse Effect

Even on a cold winter day, a greenhouse feels warm inside. Demonstrate the greenhouse effect for yourself on a sunny day.

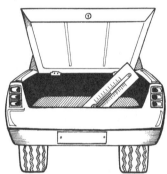

You need:
- 2 dishtowels
- 2 thermometers
- Access to an automobile

1. Roll the dishtowel up and put it on the trunk of the car. Slip one thermometer just under the last layer of the dishtowel from the top.
2. Roll the other dishtowel up and slip the other thermometer inside it the same as in step 1. Place the second dishtowel and thermometer inside the car. Roll up the car windows and leave the car undisturbed for an hour.
3. After an hour, note the temperature on both thermometers. Check again in another hour.

How much hotter is it inside the car than outside?

Venus's clouds work like the car's glass. All wavelengths of light can enter. But infrared rays, which cause heat, can't escape. That raises the temperature dramatically.

Mars takes 687 Earth days to orbit the Sun.

Like Venus, Mars has 95 percent carbon dioxide in its atmosphere. The rest is about 3 percent nitrogen and 2 percent argon. Unlike Venus, however, the atmosphere is very thin.

Mars's polar ice caps are mostly frozen carbon dioxide, or dry ice. When summer warms each Pole, some carbon dioxide changes from a solid to a vapor. It freezes again when winter returns. Mars has no liquid water on its surface. Any water on the planet lies frozen beneath the ice caps or under the surface.

In 1877, Italian astronomer Giovanni V. Schiaparelli saw lines on Mars with his telescope. He called them *canali*, meaning channels. Many English-speaking people thought he meant "canals" and wondered who built them. In fact, no one actually built canals on Mars. The lines Schiaparelli saw were likely optical illusions—tricks of the

Astronomical Numbers

Kepler's Third Law

Mathematician Johannes Kepler also figured that a planet's average distance from the Sun is related to how long it takes to orbit the sun. His formula uses the astronomical unit (AU). One AU equals Earth's average distance from the sun. That equals about 93 million miles (150 million kilometers).

Kepler's math formula (also called Kepler's third law) says: distance × distance × distance = orbit period × orbit period.

Mars takes about 1.88 years to go around the Sun. Thus, its average distance from the sun is about 1.5 AU. That means it's about 50 percent farther from the Sun than Earth is.

Use a calculator to check Kepler's third law for yourself. Here are the average distances and orbit periods in years for each planet. Multiply distance by distance by distance. Then press the square root key. The result should be close to the planet's orbit period.

Planet	Distance (in AU)	Period (in years)
Mercury	0.39	0.24
Venus	0.72	0.62
Earth	1.00	1.00
Mars	1.52	1.88
Jupiter	5.20	11.86
Saturn	9.54	29.46
Uranus	19.19	84.07
Neptune	30.06	164.80
Pluto	39.60	248.60

eye—caused by contrasts between light and dark areas.

Mars may be small, but it hosts the solar system's largest volcano. Olympus Mons is 370 miles (600 kilometers) across at its base. It rises 16 miles (25 kilometers) above the planet surface. In contrast, Mauna Loa, Earth's largest volcano, is only 6 miles (10 kilometers) high.

Mars also has tremendous canyons and valleys. Stretching nearly a fifth of the way around the planet, Valles Marineris is about

Pathfinder

Robot explorers are sent to collect data from planets where human astronauts could never survive. See if you can steer the Pathfinder rover around the rocks of Mars and back to the probe it came in.

Good Night!

An astronomer must carefully follow many steps in order to discover the secrets of the universe. You must carefully follow the directions below to learn the secret answer to the following riddle:

   When you go to bed, what does the sky turn on for you?

   HINT: As you complete each step, write the new combination of letters on the lines to the right.

1. Print the words "moon and stars" leaving out the spaces between the words. _____

2. Move the 4th letter to the 1st position. _____

3. Delete the letter R. _____

4. Change the D to an L. _____

5. Replace the 2nd and 8th letters with the letter I. _____

6. Replace both letters A with the letter G. _____

7. Change both letters O to the letter H. _____

8. Switch the 9th and the 10th letters with each other. _____

9. Switch the 4th and the 5th letters with each other. _____

10. Change the middle letter to the letter T. _____

11. Move the middle letter between the last two letters. _____

12. Change the 3rd letter to the letter T. _____

13. Take the 3rd letter and move it between the H and the L. _____

FUN FACT

Martians, Martians Everywhere

In his 1895 book, *The War of the Worlds*, writer H. G. Wells described Martians as monsters with tentacles. In a scary adventure, the Martians tried to invade Earth.

Edgar Rice Burroughs wrote 11 adventure books about Martians. In *Princess of Mars*, hero John Carter rescued beautiful Dejah Thoris from savage green men.

Arthur C. Clarke's *The Sands of Mars* talked about kangaroo-like Martians. Ray Bradbury's *The Martian Chronicles* talked about humanlike creatures who lived near watery canals.

NASA's *Mariner* missions showed how bleak the Martian terrain really is. Life as we know it certainly does not inhabit the red planet. Analyzing a Martain meteorite in 1996, NASA scientists found chemicals often left when organisms die and decay. Might the "Martians" once have been microscopic organisms?

SPACE SHUTTLE EXPLORER

2,500 miles (4,000 kilometers) long. It's about 4 miles (6 kilometers) deep and 120 miles (200 kilometers) wide. In contrast, the Grand Canyon on Earth is just over 1 mile (1.6 kilometers) deep and only about 217 miles (347 kilometers) long.

Martian Moons: Phobos and Deimos

Mars has two moons: Phobos and Deimos. Because they're so small, their gravity does not pull them into sphere shapes. Rather, they look lumpy. Phobos measures roughly 18 × 14 × 12 miles (28 × 23 × 20 kilometers). The dimensions of Deimos are about 10 × 8 × 6 miles (16 × 12 × 10 kilometers).

Photos from the *Mars Global Surveyor* show grooves on Phobos. They may have formed from the impact that created Stickney, the moon's largest crater. Or, some unknown factor might have carved the grooves.

Deimos doesn't have such grooves. Its surface also seems smoother than Phobos's. That's because a layer of fine dust lies on the moon's surface.

The small size of Mars's moons means their gravity is very weak. Suppose an athlete could jump 6 feet (2 meters) high on Earth. On Phobos, he or she would soar 1.7 miles (2.8 kilometers) above the surface!

Scientists still aren't sure how Phobos and Deimos formed. They could have come together at the same time as the planet Mars. Or, perhaps they are asteroids that were captured by Mars's gravitational field.

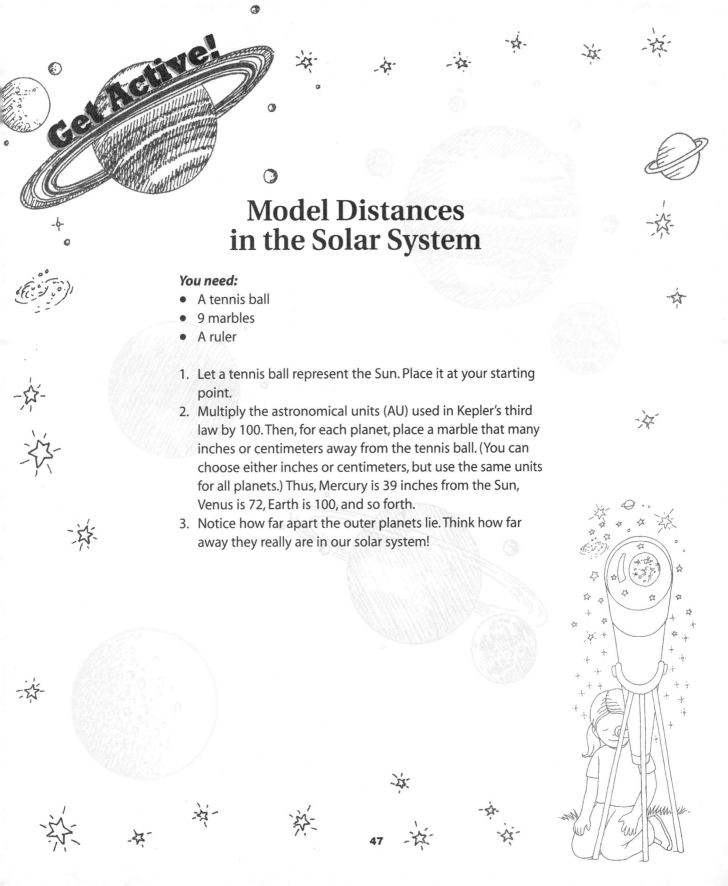

Model Distances
in the Solar System

You need:

- A tennis ball
- 9 marbles
- A ruler

1. Let a tennis ball represent the Sun. Place it at your starting point.
2. Multiply the astronomical units (AU) used in Kepler's third law by 100. Then, for each planet, place a marble that many inches or centimeters away from the tennis ball. (You can choose either inches or centimeters, but use the same units for all planets.) Thus, Mercury is 39 inches from the Sun, Venus is 72, Earth is 100, and so forth.
3. Notice how far apart the outer planets lie. Think how far away they really are in our solar system!

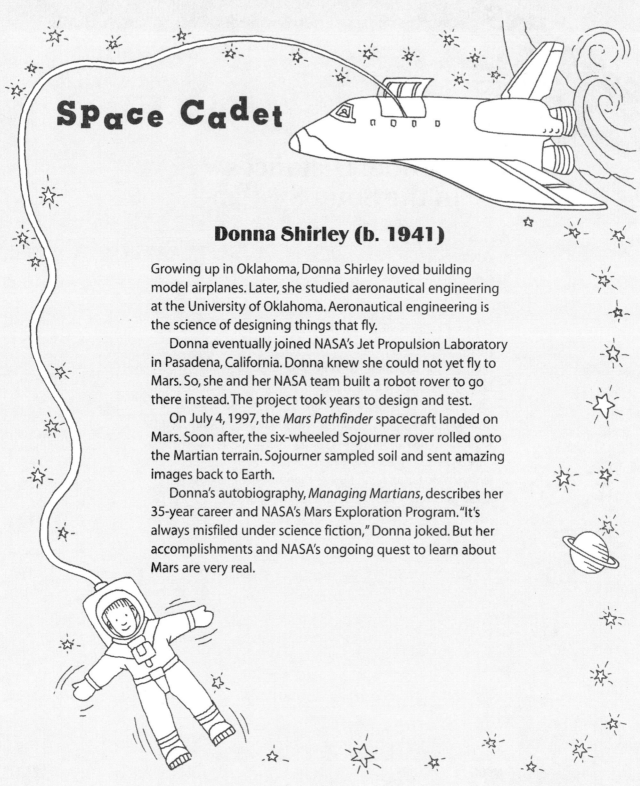

Space Cadet

Donna Shirley (b. 1941)

Growing up in Oklahoma, Donna Shirley loved building model airplanes. Later, she studied aeronautical engineering at the University of Oklahoma. Aeronautical engineering is the science of designing things that fly.

Donna eventually joined NASA's Jet Propulsion Laboratory in Pasadena, California. Donna knew she could not yet fly to Mars. So, she and her NASA team built a robot rover to go there instead. The project took years to design and test.

On July 4, 1997, the *Mars Pathfinder* spacecraft landed on Mars. Soon after, the six-wheeled Sojourner rover rolled onto the Martian terrain. Sojourner sampled soil and sent amazing images back to Earth.

Donna's autobiography, *Managing Martians*, describes her 35-year career and NASA's Mars Exploration Program. "It's always misfiled under science fiction," Donna joked. But her accomplishments and NASA's ongoing quest to learn about Mars are very real.

Is Terraforming in Our Future?

Might people live on Mars? A land-based space station could one day be built on the planet. Like the space station orbiting Earth, it would need a controlled atmosphere, water, food, and everything else to sustain life. Then colony crews could live and work at the station. To go outside and explore the planet, people would don space suits. They would drive rover vehicles over Mars's rocky terrain.

Suppose more people wanted to colonize Mars. In theory, it might be possible to make Mars more like Earth through a process called terraforming.

Right now, Mars has very low atmospheric pressure, cold temperatures, and not enough oxygen. But dark matter absorbs more heat than white matter. So, dropping dark soot or ash on Mars's ice caps should make them warmer. The warmer temperature should then melt some of the carbon dioxide that's frozen there.

When carbon dioxide melts, it goes straight from a solid to a gas in a process called sublimation. The carbon dioxide gas would go into the atmosphere and make it thicker. In theory, the gas would create a greenhouse effect and warm up the planet's surface temperatures.

It could also melt some water under the ice caps. Algae from Earth could then make some of Mars's carbon dioxide release oxygen. That oxygen then might make the atmosphere breathable.

Just because we might be able to do something, however, doesn't mean

Squiggle Giggle

Draw your own Martian using these four lines.

Draw a spaceship for your Martian using these four lines.

Mars Colony Groupie

These colonists packed in a hurry for their move to Mars. First, unscramble each group of letters to figure out what they brought to start their new colony. Then, fit each word into the grid, reading from top to bottom. When you are finished, read across the shaded letters to find the answer to this question:

What did the colonist's moms tell them to do right away when they got to Mars?

1. TCSAEUIPSS _____
2. ENACIMHS _____
3. DOFO _____
4. SLAPNT _____
5. YXEOGN _____
6. EAETRHS _____
7. ERVSRO _____
8. DEMO _____
9. EAWRT _____

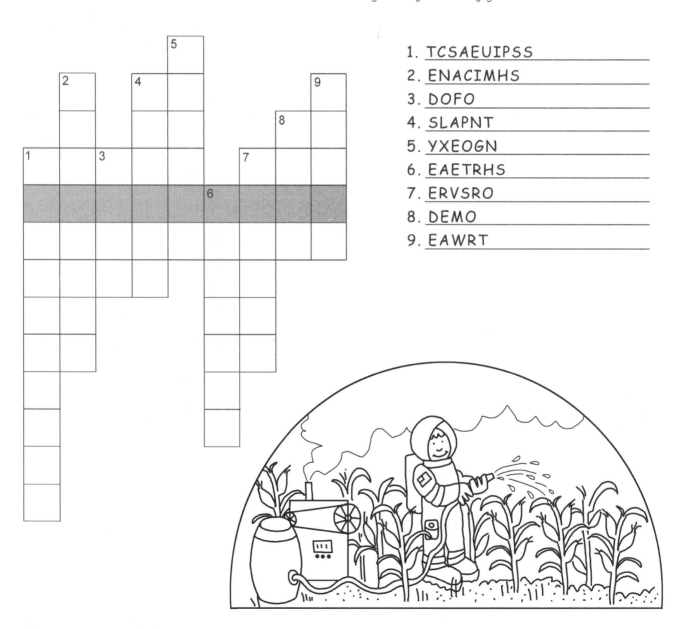

Mars Millennium Project

www.mars2030.net

See kids' ideas for establishing a 100-person community on Mars.

FUN FACT

Mars Mishaps

Two failed Mars missions in 1999 reminded people that space science still isn't perfect. The *Mars Climate Orbiter* should have gathered data about Martian weather. Instead, on September 23, 1999, the spacecraft disappeared. It may have burned up in Mars's atmosphere, broken apart, or spun away in space.

Just months later, the *Mars Polar Lander* was supposed to land safely near Mars's south pole. It too disappeared. For more than a month, NASA tried unsuccessfully to communicate with the lander. As this book goes to press, the reasons for its failure are still unknown.

Fortunately, more Mars missions are on the horizon. As the saying goes, if at first you don't succeed, try, try again.

that we should do it. We are only just learning about Mars. We don't know all the consequences that would follow if we tried to change the planet permanently. From an environmental perspective, we should probably clean up our own planet first.

Any terraforming process would also take thousands of years and be incredibly expensive. Would the end product be worth it? Or are there better things we could do right here on Earth?

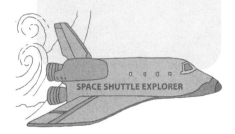

SPACE SHUTTLE EXPLORER

Draw Mars's Orbit

Planets' orbits aren't exactly circles. Rather, they're ellipses, or ovals.

Mathematically speaking, an ellipse is a closed curve around two points, called its foci (the plural of "focus"). The sum of the distances from the two foci is the same for every point on the ellipse.

German scientist Johannes Kepler (1571–1630) figured out that planet orbits were ellipses by watching Mars. Here's how to draw an ellipse.

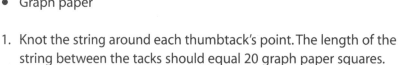

You need:

- String
- 2 thumbtacks
- Graph paper
- Newspaper
- A pencil

1. Knot the string around each thumbtack's point. The length of the string between the tacks should equal 20 graph paper squares.
2. Place the graph paper over a thick stack of newspaper. Press tacks into the graph paper 2 squares apart and hold them.
3. With your free hand, use the pencil to pull the string taut. Keeping the string taut, draw a curve around the two thumbtacks. You may need to lift the pencil and pull the string again at a few points.

Your ellipse resembles Mars's orbit. In our solar system, the Sun would be at one of the thumbtack points.

Moving the thumbtacks apart would produce a flatter ellipse. Mathematicians describe flatter ellipses as having more "eccentricity." Among the planets, Pluto and Mercury have the most eccentric orbits.

Half the distance across the longest part of its orbit is a planet's average distance from the sun. The closest point to the Sun is an orbit's perihelion. Planets travel fastest in their orbits when they are near the perihelion. Planets travel slowest when they are farthest from the sun.

CHAPTER FOUR

THE OUTER PLANETS:

JUPITER, SATURN, URANUS, NEPTUNE, AND PLUTO

Astronomical Numbers

What Would You Weigh?

All things being equal, the more mass something has, the more it weighs. Once we escape Earth's gravity, though, all things aren't equal anymore.

Weight is a relative measure of how much gravitational pull one body, such as a planet, has on something else. If a planet has a stronger gravitational pull, you would weigh more there.

Here's how much someone who weighs 100 pounds (45 kg) would weigh on other planets:

Planet	Pounds	Kilograms
Mercury	38	17
Venus	90	41
Earth	100	45
Mars	38	17
Jupiter	254	115
Saturn	116	53
Uranus	92	41
Neptune	119	55
Pluto	6	3

Giant Jupiter

Measuring 89,365 miles (142,984 kilometers) across, Jupiter is our solar system's largest planet. Over 1,400 Earths could fit inside it. It's no wonder, then, that this huge planet was named after the king of the Roman gods.

Jupiter's makeup is a lot like the Sun's. It has about 90 percent hydrogen and 10 percent helium, plus traces of other chemicals. Jupiter may be a "failed star" that never got hot enough for nuclear fusion.

Yet Jupiter's gravity is so great that its core emits heat. In fact, Jupiter's internal heat exceeds any warmth it gets from the Sun 484 million miles (778 million kilometers) away. That heat brings its average surface temperature up to −163°F (−108°C). That's still too cold for life as we know it.

Jupiter takes almost 12 years to orbit the Sun. But its days last less than 10 hours. The planet's swift spinning sets up tremendous winds.

The winds combine with heat currents in the planet's gases to produce some of the stormiest weather in the solar system.

Jupiter's Great Red Spot extends more than three times Earth's diameter across Jupiter's Southern Hemisphere. The spot is a giant storm that's been raging over 100 years.

Jupiter's Moons

Galileo Galilei was the first scientist to see any of Jupiter's moons. Using a telescope, Galileo spied Ganymede, Europa, Callisto, and Io. Since then, scientists have found a dozen more moons orbiting Jupiter.

Ganymede is the solar system's biggest moon. With a diameter of 3,210 miles (5,262 kilometers), it's larger than Mercury. Ganymede's core takes up about half its diameter. The mantle over that is probably made of ice and silica compounds. Its grooved and cratered crust seems to be mostly water ice.

Callisto has the most cratered surface of any moon in the solar system. The center of its Valhalla impact basin stretches 375 miles (600 kilometers) across. Rings surrounding the center extend the basin to 1,875 miles (3,000 kilometers) in diameter. Water ice and rock make up this dark-colored moon.

Jupiter's moon Io has about 80 volcanoes. NASA's *Galileo* spacecraft found some shooting 50 miles (75 kilometers) above Io's surface. Io has nonvolcanic mountains too. Some tower almost 10 miles (16 kilometers) high.

Billions of years ago, Earth probably had as much volcanic activity as Io has now. By studying Io, scientists hope to learn more about how Earth formed. "Io is the next best thing to traveling back in time to Earth's earlier years," said Torrence Johnson at NASA's Jet Propulsion Laboratory in Pasadena, California.

Long cracks crisscross Europa's icy surface. In January 2000, NASA's *Galileo* spacecraft found directional changes in

Jupiter's Rings

In 1979, the *Voyager 1* spacecraft gave Earth its first views of Jupiter's dark rings. The rings probably come from debris kicked up from Jupiter's moons after crashes with comets or asteroids.

SPACE SHUTTLE EXPLORER

the moon's magnetic field. Such changes wouldn't show up if Europa were a solid, icy mass. The changes do make sense, however, if something is sloshing around under the icy crusts. "I think these findings tell us that there is indeed a layer of liquid water beneath Europa's surface," announced NASA's Margaret Kivelson.

If Europa has an ocean under its icy surface, might microbes or some other organisms live there? In 1997, scientists discovered organic compounds on Callisto and Ganymede. They think these chemicals, which are needed for life, also exist on Io and Europa.

Saturn: The Ringed Planet

Named after Jupiter's father in Roman mythology, Saturn is *the* ringed planet. Jupiter, Uranus, and Neptune also have rings, but theirs are dark and drab. In contrast, Saturn's rings gleam brilliantly.

Saturn's rings measure almost 170,000 miles (272,000 kilometers) across. Their width is less than 1 mile (1.6 kilometers). Most amateur astronomers see three main rings with their telescopes. In reality, about 3,000 closely spaced rings orbit Saturn.

The rings aren't solid. Rather, they're made mostly of ice particles, plus some bits of rock. The smallest bits are the size of dust motes. The largest measure 164 feet (50 meters) across.

Saturn's rings are probably leftover material that never came together to form a moon. Now, Saturn's gravity and other forces keep the rings from joining together. Another theory holds that the rings are debris from an old moon that broke apart.

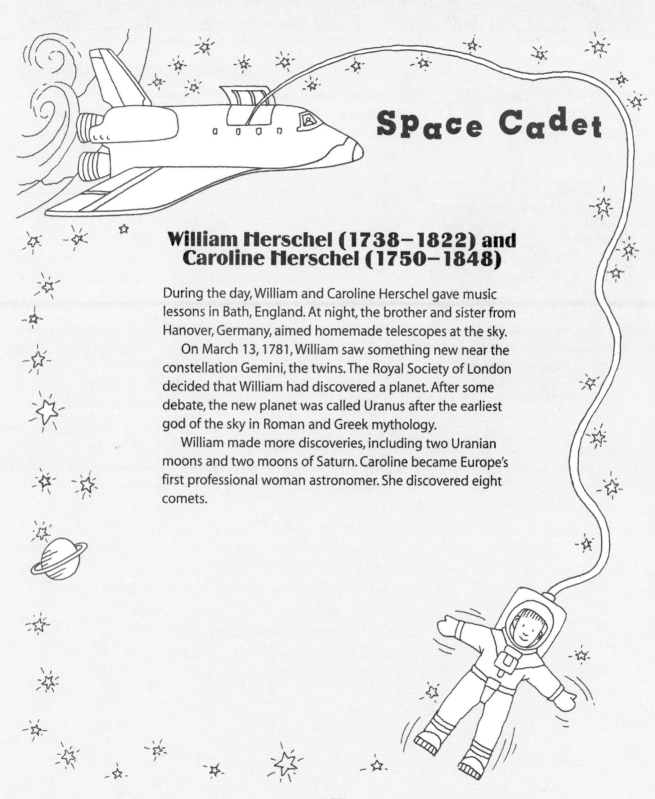

Space Cadet

William Herschel (1738–1822) and Caroline Herschel (1750–1848)

During the day, William and Caroline Herschel gave music lessons in Bath, England. At night, the brother and sister from Hanover, Germany, aimed homemade telescopes at the sky.

On March 13, 1781, William saw something new near the constellation Gemini, the twins. The Royal Society of London decided that William had discovered a planet. After some debate, the new planet was called Uranus after the earliest god of the sky in Roman and Greek mythology.

William made more discoveries, including two Uranian moons and two moons of Saturn. Caroline became Europe's first professional woman astronomer. She discovered eight comets.

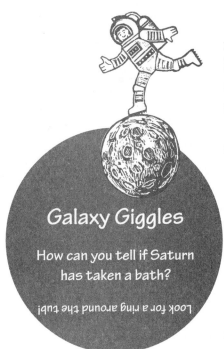

Saturn's tilt relative to Earth determines how we see its rings. During the first years of the 21st century, we have a broad view of the rings. In 2009, however, the rings will be edgewise to us and will virtually disappear. Within a couple of years, we'll see Saturn's rings again.

Saturn itself is huge. As the second largest planet, Saturn measures 75,335 miles (20,536 kilometers) across at its equator. Its volume is 744 times that of Earth. It has 95 times the mass of Earth.

However, Saturn's average density is only 0.69. That means that a cubic centimeter has less than 70 percent as much matter in it as the same volume of water. (Water equals 1.00.) If a big enough bathtub existed, Saturn could float in it.

Like Jupiter, Saturn is a gas giant. Hydrogen and helium make up most of the planet. Scientists believe there's an ocean of liquid hydrogen beneath the gas and then a dense, solid core.

Also like Jupiter, Saturn has tremendous gravity at its core. As a result, Saturn gives off more heat than it receives from the Sun. Despite that, Saturn's average surface temperature is –219°F (–139°C). Brrrr!

A year on Saturn is a long time. The planet takes 29.5 Earth years to revolve around the Sun. Saturn lies an average of 888 million miles (1.4 billion kilometers) from the Sun.

In contrast, Saturn's days zip by. One rotation takes just over 10 hours. The fast spin flattens Saturn's North and South poles. Saturn's spin also sets strong winds in motion at speeds up to 1,100 miles (1,770 kilometers) per hour. The winds stretch clouds into broad bands around Saturn.

Saturn's Moons

Saturn has 18 known moons. Titan is the largest, measuring 3,219 miles (5,150 kilometers) across. Other moons include Dione, Phoebe, Iapetus, Enceladus, and heavily cratered Tethys.

Unlike other moons in our solar system, Titan has a substantial atmosphere. Its "air" may even be like Earth's atmosphere was billions of years ago.

Titan's frozen surface wouldn't support life as we know it. But scientists wonder what might be farther down. When NASA's *Cassini* spacecraft visits Saturn in 2004, it will drop a probe through Titan's thick orange clouds.

Unusual Uranus

In Roman myths, Uranus was Saturn's father. Uranus is the third largest planet in our solar system, measuring 15,974 miles (25,559 kilometers) across at the equator. Its mass is over 14 times that of Earth.

Like Jupiter and Saturn, Uranus is made mostly of hydrogen and helium gas. Methane gas in the surface layers scatters blue light. Thus, Uranus appears blue to us. Faint rings circle Uranus. Made of dust and debris, they appear almost black.

Uranus is the "odd ball" planet in our solar system. Uranus takes only about 17 hours to rotate on its axis. But Uranus rotates from east

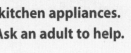

Note: **Be careful with kitchen appliances. Ask an adult to help.**

Mold a Moon

Uranus's moon Miranda has odd surface features. Use a flour-salt dough to make your own odd looking moon.

You need:

- ¾ cup (187 milliliters) flour
- ¼ cup (63 milliliters) salt
- A mixing bowl
- ¼ cup (63 milliliters) water
- ¼ cup (63 milliliters) vegetable oil
- 2 drops food coloring (optional)
- Waxed paper
- Beads
- Toothpicks
- A plastic knife
- A cuticle stick
- A cookie sheet
- Aluminum foil
- Potholders

1. Combine the flour and salt in the mixing bowl. Then add water, oil, and food coloring. Mix the ingredients to make modeling dough.
2. Working over the waxed paper, form the dough into a ball.
3. Form moon-like features on your ball. Press beads into dough and remove them to make craters. Use toothpicks to carve cracks. Use a plastic knife and a cuticle stick to sculpt canyons.
4. When you're satisfied with your "moon," place it on a cookie sheet lined with aluminum foil. Ask an adult to bake the moon at 225°F (107°C) for 1 hour. Remove it carefully from the oven with potholders. Let the moon cool thoroughly until it's hard and dry.

Of course, your moon won't go into orbit around Uranus. It will, however, make a neat paperweight. That way all your important papers won't go flying off into space!

to west—the opposite of Earth. Thus, the Sun rises in the west on Uranus—and sets in the east.

Earth's axis tilts, but our planet still spins mostly vertically with respect to the Sun. So do all other planets except Uranus. Uranus's axis tilts 98 degrees, so it spins sideways. Maybe some giant collision knocked Uranus into its skewed tilt billions of years ago.

Uranus lies about 1.8 million miles (2.9 billion kilometers) from the Sun. As it makes its 84-year trip around the Sun, Uranus's axis keeps its position in space. Thus, each pole faces the Sun at different times, and winters last 21 years. The average surface temperature on Uranus is –353°F (–215°C).

The Most Moons

Right now, Uranus holds the prize for the most known moons in the solar system. New discoveries in 1999 bring the total to 21.

One tiny moon about 31,250 miles (50,000 kilometers) above the planet's atmosphere orbits Uranus in just over 15 hours. Another newly discovered moon orbits almost 16 million miles (25 million kilometers) from the planet. Its orbit lasts about 5 years. As this book goes to press, scientists are conducting more observations that will help confirm that these bodies are in fact moons, rather than asteroids or something else.

Even before the new discoveries, Uranus's moons were remarkable. Titania, the largest moon, measures 493 miles (789 kilometers) across. It orbits Uranus 272,400 miles (436,000 kilometers) from the planet's center.

Long valleys and faults stretch along Titania's cratered surface. The fault lines suggest that the

FuN FACT

Neptune's Moons

So far, we know about eight moons orbiting Neptune. They are Triton, Nereid, Despina, Galatea, Larissa, Naiad, Proteus, and Thalassa.

Measuring 846 miles (1,353 kilometers) across, Triton is the largest moon. Made mostly of ice, Triton has a very thin atmosphere of nitrogen and methane. It travels clockwise and orbits Neptune in less than 6 days. In contrast, Nereid's 360-day orbit takes nearly a whole Earth year. Nereid lies 3.4 million miles (5.5 million kilometers) from Neptune.

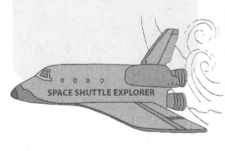

SPACE SHUTTLE EXPLORER

moon's interior may be geologically active. Ariel, Uranus's brightest moon, also has craters, valleys, and faults.

Craters on Oberon seem to have lines stretching out from them. They probably formed when debris fell back to the surface after impacts caused the craters. Oberon also features a mountain 4 miles (6.4 kilometers) high.

Miranda is an odd moon. Some parts have craters like the Moon. Other areas have deep canyons. Other regions sport strange grooves. Still another area seems to have a giant boomerang carved on it.

What made Miranda so strange? Perhaps the moon broke apart and came back together again. Or perhaps the moon's geology is very complex.

Most Uranian moons are named after characters in stories by William Shakespeare and Alexander Pope. Besides those named earlier, there are Cordelia, Ophelia, Bianca, Cressida, Juliet, Portia, Puck, Belinda, Rosalind, Umbriel, and Desdemona. If you could name a moon for a story character, who would you pick?

Neptune: A Stormy Planet

Neptune completes one rotation every 19 hours. This is incredibly fast when you factor in Neptune's diameter of 30,782 miles (49,251 kilometers). Just thinking about it can make you dizzy!

In contrast, Neptune takes its time orbiting the Sun. One Neptune year equals 165 Earth years.

Scientists believe Neptune has a hot rocky core, covered with an ocean of water and other chemicals. The top layer of the ocean seems to merge into the planet's atmosphere. The atmosphere is mainly hydrogen and helium.

The high heat inside Neptune causes convection currents. Heat tends to rise and cooler matter falls. Neptune's surface probably gets as much heat from its central core as it does from the Sun. Yet the planet's average surface temperature is –355°F (–229°C). That's cold.

Pressure differences in Neptune's atmosphere cause winds. The winds interact with Neptune's rapid spinning and cause stormy weather. One dark storm area photographed by the *Voyager 2* spacecraft was larger than the diameter of Earth.

Sunlight scattering through Neptune's upper atmosphere gives the planet a blue appearance. Small amounts of methane gas add to the blue color. Perhaps that is why this planet was named after the Roman god of the sea.

The Search for Pluto

During the 1800s, scientists calculated orbits for Uranus and Neptune. But the planets didn't quite follow the calculated paths. Was gravity from something else pulling on the planets?

Percival Lowell (1855–1916) wanted to find "Planet X." Starting in 1905, Lowell and his assistants took nearly 500 pairs of photographs at the Lowell Observatory in Arizona.

Photos in each pair showed the same part of the sky, but they were taken at different times. Scientists compared the photos, using a machine called a Blink-Microscope-Comparator. Lowell reasoned that if any object shifted from one photo to another, it would be a planet.

Lowell died without finding Planet X. In 1929, Clyde Tombaugh resumed the search. After months of tedious work, he found one dim object that had shifted in photos taken on January 23 and 29, 1930. "That's it!" thought Tombaugh excitedly.

FUN FACT

Who Found Neptune?

Oddities in Uranus's orbit suggested a planet farther out might be pulling at it. Working independently, England's John Couch Adams (1819–1892) and France's Urbain Leverrier (1811–1877) used math to predict Neptune's position in 1845 and 1846, respectively. Not until autumn 1846 did astronomers Johann Galle (1812–1910) and Heinrich d'Arrest (1822–1875) check out Leverrier's prediction.

So, who found Neptune? The best answer is that it took several people.

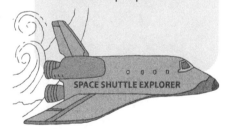

SPACE SHUTTLE EXPLORER

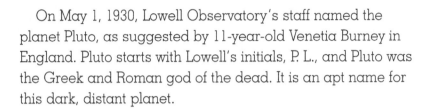

On May 1, 1930, Lowell Observatory's staff named the planet Pluto, as suggested by 11-year-old Venetia Burney in England. Pluto starts with Lowell's initials, P. L., and Pluto was the Greek and Roman god of the dead. It is an apt name for this dark, distant planet.

Pluto: A Tiny Planet

Measuring only 1,410 miles (2,260 kilometers) in diameter, Pluto is the smallest planet. It's even smaller than Earth's Moon.

At 3.6 billion miles (5.9 billion kilometers) from the Sun, Pluto is also the darkest and coldest planet. The warmest it ever gets is about –350°F (–175°C).

Because it's so far from the Sun, Pluto takes 248 Earth years to make one trip around the sun. Instead of lying "straight," Pluto's orbit is skewed. Think of the rest of the solar system's plane as the surface of water in a sink. Then tilt a plate halfway in the water. That's what Pluto's orbit is like.

Most of the time, Pluto is the farthest planet from the Sun. From 1977 to 1999, however, Pluto's tilted orbit brought it closer to the Sun than Neptune. Don't worry about a collision, though. Because of the tilt, Pluto and Neptune are still 240 million miles apart where their orbits "cross."

Most of Pluto's surface is frozen nitrogen and methane. There may also be frozen ethane, water, and ammonia, as well as rock.

Pluto may be dark and dismal, but it's not alone. In 1978, Lowell Observatory scientists discovered Pluto's moon, Charon. Oddly, Charon's orbit around Pluto takes about as long as Pluto's day—6 days and 9 hours of Earth time. Thus, if someone stood on Pluto's surface, Charon would seem to stand still in the sky. Pluto and Charon also seem to swing around each other.

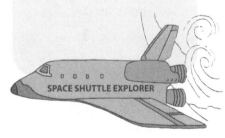

SPACE SHUTTLE EXPLORER

FUN FACT

Neptune's Rings: Raising Eyebrows

Some of Neptune's dark, narrow rings have gaps that make them look like orbiting eyebrows. Scientists first thought that Neptune's moon, Galatea, pulled some of the ring material apart. A newer theory suggests that the rings may be the remains of a moon destroyed by meteor impacts. If so, the arcs may be a halfway step before the debris forms whole rings.

Can You Get There From Here?

It could take thousands of years to travel from one place in space to another—can you make the journey in only a few steps? Use the lines provided to write out how you would change the letters in the word on the left to make it into the word on the right. You can only make one change in each step.

Go from HERE to THERE in one step.

1. _____

Go from SHUTTLE to HUBBLE in two steps.

1. _____

2. _____

Go from EARTH to MARS in three steps.

1. _____

2. _____

3. _____

Go from URANUS to SATURN in four steps.

1. _____

2. _____

3. _____

4. _____

KEY: Each of the following changes equals one step:

- Add or delete a letter
- Change the position of a letter
- Switch two letters with each other
- Reverse the whole word

Seeing Pluto from Earth requires a telescope. Check astronomy magazines and star maps to find out when it will be visible in the sky. If you're going to look for Pluto, though, look soon. Pluto was closest to Earth in 1999. For more than 100 years, Pluto's orbit will carry it farther and farther away.

Demoting Pluto?

Pluto is small, but does that mean it's not a planet? Strangely enough, that's just what some scientists suggested in 1998 and 1999.

Some people, like Brian Marsden at the Harvard-Smithsonian Center for Astrophysics in Massachusetts, wanted to give Pluto a "dual designation," as both a planet and a "minor planet." Others suggested Pluto should be called a "trans-Neptunian object," like the 100 new "things" found beyond Neptune since 1992.

While scientists debated the issues, the public responded. Pluto, it turns out, has lots of fans. For now, Pluto is still a planet.

Meanwhile, scientists are pondering other questions. Pluto's small size isn't enough to pull on the orbits of Neptune and Uranus. If that's true, do Neptune and Uranus just naturally have weird orbits? Did they form much closer to Jupiter and Saturn and then somehow get "pushed" into their present orbits by the gravity fields of those planets? Or is another mystery planet still out there?

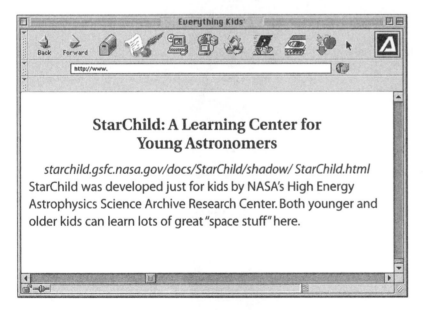

StarChild: A Learning Center for Young Astronomers

starchild.gsfc.nasa.gov/docs/StarChild/shadow/ StarChild.html
StarChild was developed just for kids by NASA's High Energy Astrophysics Science Archive Research Center. Both younger and older kids can learn lots of great "space stuff" here.

CHAPTER FIVE

ASTEROIDS, COMETS, AND METEORS

The Asteroid Belt

On New Year's Day in 1801, Italian astronomer Giuseppe Piazzi (1746–1826) aimed his telescope at the constellation Taurus the Bull. One faint object wasn't on any of his star maps. Over several nights, the object changed its position relative to the other stars. It didn't seem like a comet. Might it be another planet?

Piazzi's discovery lies about 259 million miles (414 million kilometers) from the Sun. That puts it between the planets Mars and Jupiter. Piazzi named it Ceres, after the daughter of Saturn in Roman myths.

At first people thought Ceres was indeed a planet, but its diameter is only 584 miles (934 kilometers). Ceres could fit inside Jupiter over 3 million times. Could something so small be a planet?

Then astronomers found other objects orbiting the Sun between Mars and Jupiter. In 1802, for example, Heinrich Olbers (1758–1810) discovered an object he called Pallas. Its diameter was 329 miles (526 kilometers). In 1804, Karl Harding (1765–1834) discovered Juno, which measured 168 miles (268 kilometers) across. In 1807, Olbers found another object called Vesta, with a diameter of 319 miles (510 kilometers).

Eventually, scientists discovered thousands of similar objects orbiting the Sun. William Herschel (see Space Cadet on page 57) coined the name **asteroids** for the objects.

Ceres is the largest asteroid discovered so far. The smallest asteroids are not even as big as a football field. Some asteroids are spheres, but most have odd shapes. Reach into a sack of potatoes and lay any six on a table. Their bizarre bumps and lumps are the shape of "typical" asteroids.

The rocky material in the asteroids is about 4.6 billion years old—as old as our solar system. Scientists aren't sure how the asteroids got to be the odd orbiting bodies they are today. One

FUN FACT

Why Did Dinosaurs Become Extinct?

Scientists believe a large comet or asteroid killed off the giant dinosaurs and most other large life forms that roamed Earth 65 million years ago. They estimate that the comet or asteroid was about 6 miles (10 kilometers) wide. The Chicxulub crater from that impact lies underwater off the shore of Central America.

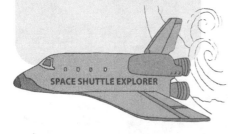

SPACE SHUTTLE EXPLORER

theory is that the asteroids are bits and pieces that never quite came together to form a planet. Another theory is that the asteroids are debris left from a catastrophic collision in the solar system. If a planet once orbited the Sun between Mars and Jupiter, the asteroid belt may be all that remains of it.

A Collision Course?

Not all asteroids stay in the asteroid belt. Many small asteroids, called Near-Earth Asteroids, come within 30 million miles (45 million kilometers) of Earth. Could one of them be on a collision course with our planet?

In February 2000, astronomers sounded the alarm. They'd found an asteroid with a one-in-a-million chance of crashing into Earth in the year 2022. Just one day later, however, they said not to worry. The asteroid, 2000BF19, wouldn't hit Earth in 2022 or at any other time in the foreseeable future.

In 1996, one asteroid came within 280,000 miles of Earth. That seems far away, but astronomers considered the event a near miss from a collision.

If a sizable asteroid or other body crashed into Earth, the results would be disastrous. The impact's force would outstrip any nuclear bombs. Dust would block out sunlight and cause freezing temperatures. Mass flooding would also occur. Life as we know it would be mostly wiped out.

Should we worry about asteroids? Each Near-Earth Asteroid has about a ½ percent chance of colliding with Earth in the next million years. Previously, scientists guessed there were between 1,000 and 2,000 Near-Earth Asteroids at least 0.6 miles (1 kilometers) in diameter. Those would be large enough to cause significant destruction.

Using those numbers, scientists had said the risk of catastrophic collision with an asteroid was 1 percent in the next

FUN FACT

Halley's at Hastings

The Bayeux Tapestry in France celebrates the Norman Conquest of England at the Battle of Hastings in 1066. The giant fabric picture shows lots of soldiers, horses, and other figures, including the victorious William the Conqueror. The tapestry also shows a glowing ball with a tail in the sky. Sure enough, Halley's Comet made one of its visits in 1066. Perhaps medieval people felt the comet played a role in the Normans' decisive victory.

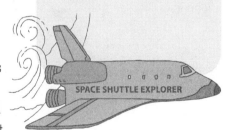

SPACE SHUTTLE EXPLORER

SPACE SHUTTLE EXPLORER

thousand years. Thanks to improved surveying, scientists now say there are only about half the number of Near-Earth Asteroids that size, or between 500 and 1,000. "This new analysis reduces by half the estimated number of these potential hazards to Earth," announced NASA's Steven Pravdo in an early 2000 press release from NASA.

In other words, don't lie awake at night worrying about an asteroid collision. As Yale University professor David Rabinowitz said in the same press release, "None of the asteroids we've observed will hit Earth anytime in the near future."

Comets

"Astronomers Say New **Comet** May Be Brightest in Decades," read the headline for a March 1996 story in the *New York Times*. The story celebrated Comet Hyakutake's appearance in the night sky.

A year later, *Newsweek*'s cover story announced, "The Return of the Great Comet." Comet Hale-Bopp was now visible in the night sky.

Comets appear in the sky as glowing balls of light, followed by giant gleaming tails. No wonder they make headlines. They are an amazing sight.

Comets are chunks of rock and ice that orbit the Sun. Unlike asteroids, they follow huge elliptical orbits. Their paths range from near the Sun to the solar system's outer reaches.

Scientists believe comets are leftovers from when the

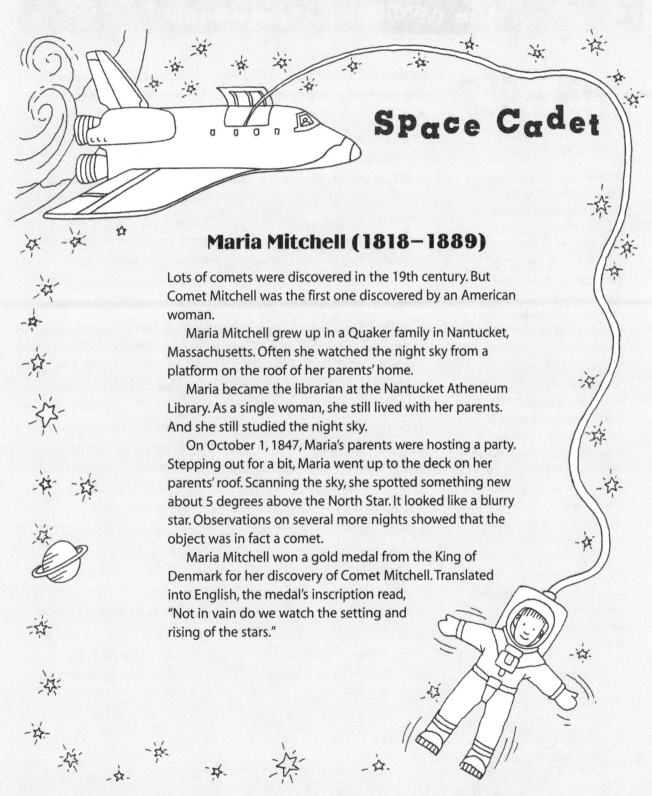

Space Cadet

Maria Mitchell (1818–1889)

Lots of comets were discovered in the 19th century. But Comet Mitchell was the first one discovered by an American woman.

Maria Mitchell grew up in a Quaker family in Nantucket, Massachusetts. Often she watched the night sky from a platform on the roof of her parents' home.

Maria became the librarian at the Nantucket Atheneum Library. As a single woman, she still lived with her parents. And she still studied the night sky.

On October 1, 1847, Maria's parents were hosting a party. Stepping out for a bit, Maria went up to the deck on her parents' roof. Scanning the sky, she spotted something new about 5 degrees above the North Star. It looked like a blurry star. Observations on several more nights showed that the object was in fact a comet.

Maria Mitchell won a gold medal from the King of Denmark for her discovery of Comet Mitchell. Translated into English, the medal's inscription read, "Not in vain do we watch the setting and rising of the stars."

FUN FACT

planets formed over 4.5 billion years ago. Many of these left-overs orbit the Sun in the Oort cloud. The Oort cloud is a collection of icy bodies at the solar system's edges. When some of these icy bodies get pulled into the inner solar system, they become comets.

When comets are in the outer reaches of their orbits, they are basically chunks of rock and ice. This main part is called the nucleus. The nucleus is rarely more than a few dozen miles or kilometers in diameter. Besides rock and dust, comets also contain some organic materials needed for life.

A cloud of gas and dust surrounds the nucleus. It's called the coma and can stretch over 60,000 miles (100,000 kilometers) across.

As the comet gets closer to the Sun, heat makes some of the ice melt and distorts the coma. The solar wind "blows" released dust and gas into giant tails. The gas tail usually looks more wispy and stretches out farther than the dust tail.

Comet tails always point away from the Sun, and they grow longer as distance from the Sun decreases. When seen from Earth, comet tails stretch for millions of miles.

Comets don't fly by Earth often. The time it takes for a comet to complete its elongated orbit is called its period. Some comets have fairly short periods. An example is Comet Wild 2, whose orbit is just over 6 years. It should swing by in 2003.

Other comets have longer periods. Seeing them is a once-in-a-lifetime event. Halley's Comet has a period of 76 years. It last flew by Earth in 1986. Comet Swift-Tuttle's period is 135 years. Its last visit was in 1992.

Still other comets have immensely long periods. Before 1997, Comet Hale-Bopp's last pass by Earth had been around 2213 B.C. At that time, pharaohs ruled over ancient Egypt.

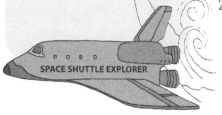

SPACE SHUTTLE EXPLORER

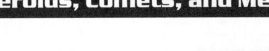

Comet Hale-Bopp's next visit won't be until around 4377. The return visit will take place sooner than the last visit. That's because gravity from Jupiter and other planets tugs at the comet's orbit.

Comet Hyakutake visits even less frequently. Don Yeomans at NASA's Jet Propulsion Laboratory estimated that the comet last passed near Earth and the Sun over 17,000 years before its 1996 discovery by Japan's Yuji Hyakutake. It may not be back for over 29,000 years. "If many people could enjoy that comet," says Hyakutake, "that is the happiest thing for me."

The Great Comet Crash

In July 1994, humans got their first glimpse of a cosmic crash in our solar system. From July 9 through July 22, bits of Comet Shoemaker-Levy 9 crashed into the planet Jupiter.

When Eugene and Carolyn Shoemaker and David Levy first discovered the comet on March 24, 1993, it had an odd "string of pearls" appearance. The year before, the comet had come too close to Jupiter. Uneven gravity pulls on the nucleus's near and far sides ripped it apart in July 1992. The nucleus became a straight trail of fragments.

Gravity from the giant planet also pulled Comet Shoemaker-Levy 9 out of its solar orbit. The comet began to swing around Jupiter. Finally, as telescopes from Earth were trained on Jupiter, 21 fragments of the comet crashed into the planet.

For a comet to break into pieces is rare. For a planet to capture a comet in orbit is even more rare. Rarest of all was the astronomers' chance to observe what happens when a large comet collides with a planet.

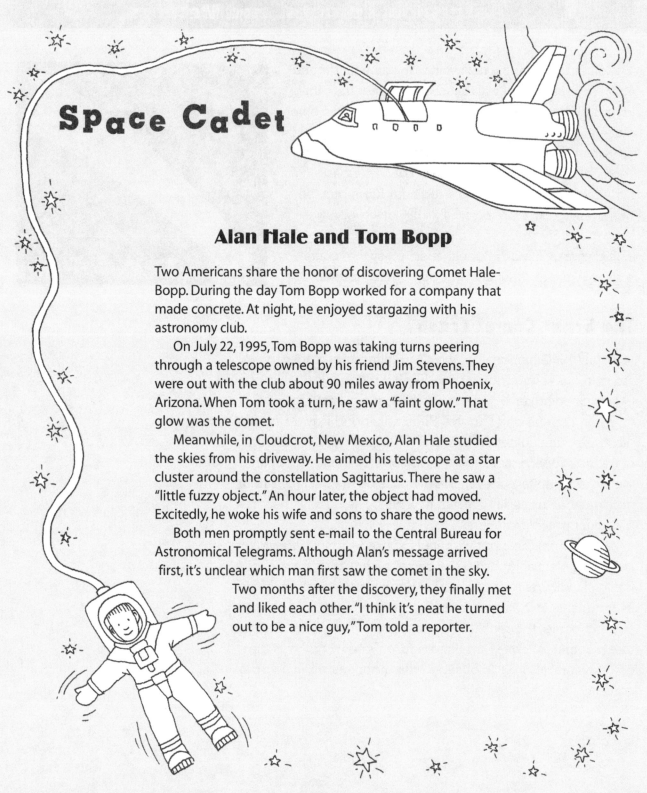

Space Cadet

Alan Hale and Tom Bopp

Two Americans share the honor of discovering Comet Hale-Bopp. During the day Tom Bopp worked for a company that made concrete. At night, he enjoyed stargazing with his astronomy club.

On July 22, 1995, Tom Bopp was taking turns peering through a telescope owned by his friend Jim Stevens. They were out with the club about 90 miles away from Phoenix, Arizona. When Tom took a turn, he saw a "faint glow." That glow was the comet.

Meanwhile, in Cloudcrot, New Mexico, Alan Hale studied the skies from his driveway. He aimed his telescope at a star cluster around the constellation Sagittarius. There he saw a "little fuzzy object." An hour later, the object had moved. Excitedly, he woke his wife and sons to share the good news.

Both men promptly sent e-mail to the Central Bureau for Astronomical Telegrams. Although Alan's message arrived first, it's unclear which man first saw the comet in the sky.

Two months after the discovery, they finally met and liked each other. "I think it's neat he turned out to be a nice guy," Tom told a reporter.

Meteor Madness

About 10 tons of material showers Earth from space every day. Fortunately, Earth's atmosphere defends the planet from these alien invaders.

The "space stuff" hurtling toward Earth is called meteoroids. Some of it is comet dust and debris. Other material comes from bits of asteroids that flew too close to Earth's gravity field. Still more is spewed into space when impacts create craters on other planets or moons.

When meteoroids strike Earth's atmosphere, they become **meteors**. Friction between the meteor and the upper atmosphere produces tremendous heat. As the meteor burns, it lights up. We see the meteor as a flashy streak across the sky. Because the streak comes and goes in an instant, many people also call meteors "shooting stars."

Most times, the meteor burns completely, leaving only dust to settle slowly to the ground. Sometimes, a hunk remains and plops onto the ground. These space rocks are called meteorites. Often they look like dark rocks. If rocks contain lots of silica, the heat might change them into pieces of glass called tektites.

Most meteors and meteorite impacts are harmless. Occasionally, though, they make a big blast. On January 18, 2000, military satellites detected a huge explosion over Canada's Yukon. It was not a bomb, but a giant meteor exploding at 80,000 feet (24 kilometers) above sea level. The

> **WORDS to KNOW**
>
> **meteor:** a body of matter from space that's heated by friction and glows as it falls through Earth's atmosphere. The body is a *meteoroid* before it enters Earth's atmosphere. Anything that survives to land on the ground is called a *meteorite*. [MEE-tee-or]

Astronomical Numbers

Dust, Dust, and More Dust!

Dust from meteors adds about 40,000 tons (19,000 tonnes) per year to Earth's mass. Next time you clean your room, perhaps you'll vacuum some space dust off the floor.

Don't Worry!

The odds that a meteorite will strike you this year are about 10 trillion to one. Although an Italian monk was supposedly killed by a meteorite in 1511, that report was never proven. More recently, in 1954, Mrs. E. Hullit Hodges was hit in the leg when a meteorite crashed into her living room. She survived and recovered just fine.

Splat!

Arizona's Barringer Meteorite Crater is ¾ mile (1.2 kilometers) wide. The iron meteor that crashed into Earth here was roughly 300 feet (90 meters) in diameter. That's the length of a football field. The meteorite struck with the force of a 3-megaton hydrogen bomb.

explosion had the force of between 2,000 and 3,000 tons of dynamite.

An even bigger blast shook Siberia in 1908. A meteor about 100 feet (30 meters) across exploded with the force of 20 million tons of dynamite. Trees and other plants within 9 miles (14 kilometers) were incinerated.

Shower Time

You can see a meteor on almost any clear night. After all, our planet is constantly being pelted with debris from outer space. But the best meteor shows occur at set times of the year, called meteor showers. Meteor showers are periods when Earth's orbit takes it through an especially heavy trail of debris. Often, the debris is left over from the path of a comet.

How good a meteor shower is depends on its parent comet. August's Perseids shower is caused by debris from Comet Swift-Tuttle. The comet's debris is

Note: Always bring an adult along for safety.

Watch a Meteor Shower

Most years, the Perseids, Geminids, and Quandrantids have the most meteors per hour. But other showers offer enjoyable viewing too.

Shower	Dates	Peak
Quadrantids	January 1–6	January 4
Lyrids	April 20–22	April 22
(Eta) Aquarids	May 2–7	May 4
(Delta) Aquarids	July 26–31	July 30
Perseids	August 10–18	August 12
Orionids	October 20–23	October 21
Taurids	November 1–7	November 4
Leonids	November 14–19	November 16
Geminids	December 7-15	December 14

Here are some tips for planning your meteor watching adventure:
1. Plan ahead. Most meteors appear after midnight. Take a nap so you'll feel rested and awake. Check the weather report too. You won't see anything if clouds cover the sky.
2. Think dark. Try to get as far away from city lights as possible.
3. Bring blankets and dress warmly. Even in summer, nights get chilly.
4. Plan to be comfortable. Bring lightweight lawn chairs. Or, spread a waterproof tarp and blankets on the ground.
5. Bring refreshments. A thermos of hot cocoa goes really well with cookies or other snacks. Remember to clean up afterward.
6. Keep an hourly count. In between spotting meteors, see what constellations and other objects you can identify in the night sky.

spread over a broad distance, so the meteor shower puts on a great show almost every year.

In contrast, November's Leonids shower is associated with Comet Tempel-Tuttle. Because that comet's debris is more "bunched up," the Leonids provide a major meteor display only every 33 years or so. Most years, watchers see only about half a dozen meteors. At the Leonids' peaks in 1998 and 1999, however, some observers saw hundreds of meteors each hour. For the 1966 Leonids shower, some reports even topped 1,000 per hour.

Meteor Missiles

At one time or another, all the planets in our solar system have been hit by meteors. So have the moons! This time, just a few names have been broken up. Use only straight lines to finish the letters and figure out what has been hit.

CHAPTER SIX

STARS AND GALAXIES

WORDS to KNOW

star: a shining globe of gas that makes energy by nuclear fusion.

Constellations in the Night Sky

Gazing at the night sky, ancient people grouped different **stars** together. Connecting the dots, they formed pictures called constellations.

When we see constellations today, it seems as though ancient people had wild imaginations. Sagittarius, for example, is visible in North America from July through September. The Greeks and Romans thought this group of stars in the southern sky looked like someone shooting arrows. When we connect its eight stars, Sagittarius looks like a teapot. Likewise, the springtime constellation Boötes looks like a starry kite instead of a herdsman.

Today, astronomers use 88 constellations to divide the sky into different areas. Constellation names are Latin, but many individual star names come from Arabic.

Where you are on Earth determines what constellations you see. People in the United States, for example, never see the Southern Cross. That constellation is visible only from the Southern Hemisphere. In contrast, people in Australia never see Polaris, or the North Star. That star in Ursa Minor, or the Little Dipper, can only be seen from the Northern Hemisphere.

Other star constellations appear only at certain times of the year. Learn more about the constellations. You'll enjoy looking for them as you stargaze in different seasons.

Some Common Constellations

Look for these constellations as you stargaze in the United States or Canada. You may want to get a star map at your library or from an astronomy magazine. Star maps show what should be in the sky at a specific date and time. They also show the relative positions of different constellations.

The Big Dipper

This group of seven bright stars seems to form a dipping cup for collecting water. It's part of the constellation Ursa Major, or the Big Bear. The dipper's handle is the bear's tail, and the cup is part of its body. Fainter stars make up the bear's chest, head, and legs.

Ursa Major and certain other star groups are circumpolar constellations. Throughout the year, they appear to rotate around the North Star—a star that is presently "lined up" with Earth's North Pole.

Face north on a clear night, and you should spot the Big Dipper. In spring, look for the Big Dipper to be upside-down, as if it's dumping water onto Polaris. In summer, the dipper's bottom appears on the left. In fall, look for the Big Dipper to be right side up and "underneath" the North Star. In winter, the dipper's bottom will lie to the right.

The Little Dipper

This northern constellation is called Ursa Minor, or the Little Bear. Find it using two "pointer stars" in the cup of the Big Dipper. Then the tip of the handle, Polaris, can help you find your way on a dark night.

Cepheus

Cepheus is supposed to be a king. Two stars represent his torso. Two stars connect for his arm and hand. One star, called Er Rai, is his knee. To us, Cepheus looks more like the outline of a house, with Er Rai as the top of the roof.

Cepheus's star, Delta Cephei, changes brightness and size every 5½ days. Its color varies too, between yellow and orange. Stars like Delta Cephei that pulsate this way are called Cepheids. Their periods vary from 1 to 50 days.

North Star Navigation

You can make a simple instrument, called an astrolabe, to tell how far north or south of the equator you are.

You need:

- A pencil
- Flexible poster board
- A compass for drawing circles
- A protractor
- A straight pin
- 2 straws
- Clay
- Tape
- Scissors
- A ruler
- A flashlight

1. Draw a dot on the poster board. Place the compass point on the dot and set the radius to 4 inches (10 centimeters). Draw a semicircle with that radius on the poster board. Draw a line through the dot along the diameter of the semicircle.

2. Place the corner point of the protractor over the dot. With a pencil, mark dots at 5-degree intervals from 5 to 90 degrees.

3. Using the ruler, draw lines from the center dot through each 5-degree mark. Extend the lines to the edge of the semicircle. Make the lines for 10, 20, 30, and so on darker than the other lines. Label numbers of degrees near the edge of the semicircle.

4. Put the compass point on the dot again. Extend the radius an extra ½ inch (1 centimeters). Draw a second semicircle beyond the first, so your number markings are inside its border.

5. Using the ruler, draw another line about ½ inch (1 centimeter) below the semicircle's diameter. Also draw a line ½ inch (1 centimeter) away from and parallel to the 90-degree line you drew in step 3.

6. Cut along the lines drawn in steps 4 and 5. Insert the straight pin through each of two straws about ½ inch (1 centimeter) from the end. Then insert the pin through the dot that was the center of your semicircle. Don't squish the straws. Attach clay to the sharp end of the pin so it won't stick you.

7. Tape one of the straws in place along the base line of your astrolabe. Also wrap tape over the clay to help it stay in place. One straw should remain movable.

8. Use your astrolabe on a clear night. Look through the taped straw toward the horizon. Then adjust the movable straw until it points to the North Star. Hold that straw in place against the curved edge.

9. Use a flashlight to read the number along the edge. That tells your approximate latitude north of the equator. One degree of latitude is 1/360 of Earth's north-south circumference, or about 70 miles.

Pictures In The Stars

Ancient people used their imagination to connect the stars into pictures of people and animals. Using a white gel pen, or white crayon, connect the numbered stars to find a modern constellation.

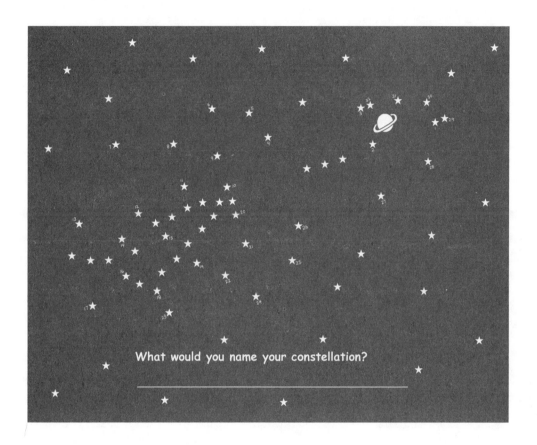

What would you name your constellation?

_____

Cassiopeia

The Greeks imagined that Cepheus's wife, Cassiopeia, sat enthroned in the sky. In one story, she boasted about her beauty. To punish her vanity, the sea god Poseidon supposedly sent a sea monster to attack the kingdom.

Two stars represent Cassiopeia's shoulders. Others are her hip, knee, and foot. To us, Cassiopeia looks like a giant W.

In areas north of 40 degrees latitude, Cassiopeia seems to rotate around Polaris throughout the year. During the spring the W appears upright. In fall, it seems upside down.

Find Cassiopeia by following the "pointer stars" at the end of the cup in the Big Dipper through Polaris. Keep going, and you'll come to Caph. Caph is a star at the right end of Cassiopeia's giant W.

Draco

In Greek and Roman myths, Draco was a dragon. Hercules killed Draco to get the golden apples it guarded.

Draco indeed resembles a dragon. Imagine a huge dragon figure carried in a Chinese New Year's Day parade. Then look in the sky between the bowls of the Big Dipper and the Little Dipper. You'll find the tip of Draco's tail.

Follow Draco's body as it snakes around the bowl of the Little Dipper. Then curve away and toward the four stars that make up the dragon's head.

Orion

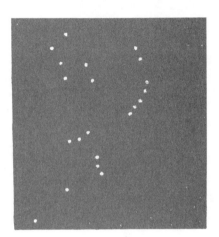

Orion, the Hunter, is easy to spot on clear winter nights. Look for a line of three bright stars, and you have Orion's belt.

Bright stars beneath the belt represent Orion's knees. The bright blue star Rigel marks his left foot. Other stars mark Orion's shoulders, neck, and arms. The bright red star Betelgeuse (pronounced "beetle juice") marks Orion's right shoulder.

Leading away from Orion's belt is his sword. To the naked eye, it looks like a misty patch. In this area of the sky is the Orion Nebula, also called the Great Nebula or M42. The nebula is a stellar nursery. New stars form from its gas.

Canis Major

Orion is supposed to be a hunter, so it's no surprise that the ancient Greeks saw Canis Major as his hunting dog. Look for it close to Orion in the winter sky. The bright star, Sirius, represents the dog's head. Other stars are its body, tail, and legs.

The Summer Triangle

As its name suggests, the Summer Triangle is formed by three bright stars. Look up near the highest point in the sky on

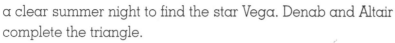

a clear summer night to find the star Vega. Denab and Altair complete the triangle.

Vega is also a star in the constellation Lyra, the lyre. Six stars represent the musical instrument and its strings.

Pegasus

In Greek mythology, Pegasus was a winged horse. Look north on a clear autumn night. Try to spot this figure flying upside down.

First, find a square of bright stars. These stars are called Alpheratz, Scheat, Algenib, and Markab. They form what astronomers call the Great Square. Other stars are Pegasus's neck, head, and hooves.

Lines of stars lead off from Alpheratz to form part of the constellation Andromeda. Greek and Roman myths said Andromeda, the princess, was Cepheus and Cassiopeia's daughter. She married Perseus, who saved her from the sea monster, Cetus.

Look carefully and you may be able to spot a patch of light near the princess Andromeda's legs. The Andromeda Galaxy, also known as M31, is the farthest thing you can see with the naked eye. Although it's the closest galaxy to our own Milky Way, the Andromeda Galaxy is still over 2 million light-years away.

Leo

Leo looked like a lion to the ancient Greeks and Romans. Six stars in Leo appear to form a backward question mark. They make up the lion's head. The bottom of the question mark is the star Regulus, 85 light-years away.

To the left of the backward question mark, three more stars form a triangle. These stars represent the lion's hindquarters.

Leo, the Lion, is one of 12 constellations that make up the zodiac. During springtime, look for Leo in the southern sky.

FUN FACT

The Zodiac

The zodiac is a group of 12 constellations. Throughout the year, the Sun's path seems to travel through where these constellations appear in the sky.

People who believe in astrology think the Sun's position in relation to the zodiac constellations influences their lives. But astrology is not a science. Astronomers, who are scientists, study the zodiac constellations and others to learn more about our universe.

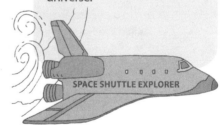

SPACE SHUTTLE EXPLORER

The Milky Way and Other Galaxies

Our Sun is just one among billions of stars in the Milky Way. The Milky Way is a galaxy—a vast collection of stars, dust, gas, and empty space.

To see the Milky Way, you need a really dark, clear night. The Milky Way appears as a hazy band. Stretching across the sky, it passes almost directly overhead. What you're seeing isn't a cloud. It's the added effects of hundreds of billions of stars.

The Milky Way is shaped like a flattened spiral. In other words, if you could view it from above, it would look like a spiral. If you could see it edge-on, it would look like a disk with a bulge in the middle. The Milky Way's diameter is about 75,000 light-years.

At our galaxy's center is an immense number of stars. Scientists also think there could be a gigantic black hole there. (Black holes are discussed more on page 95.)

Curving "arms" of stars stretch outward from the Milky Way's dense center. The curves occur because the galaxy rotates around its center. Stars become less tightly packed as the arms extend farther out. Our Sun's galaxy address is about two-thirds of the way along an arm. It's 27,710 light years from the Milky Way's center.

Some other galaxies, like the Andromeda Galaxy, are also shaped like spirals. Others have elliptical shapes. Still others have irregular shapes.

Deep-space images from the Hubble Space Telescope show an immense number of galaxies. Scientists believe there are at least 50 billion galaxies in the universe.

Galaxies contain almost all the mass that we see in the universe. But there is also matter that we can't directly see, called

Galaxy Giggles

What kind of boat would you need to cross the Sea of Tranquility?

A space ship!

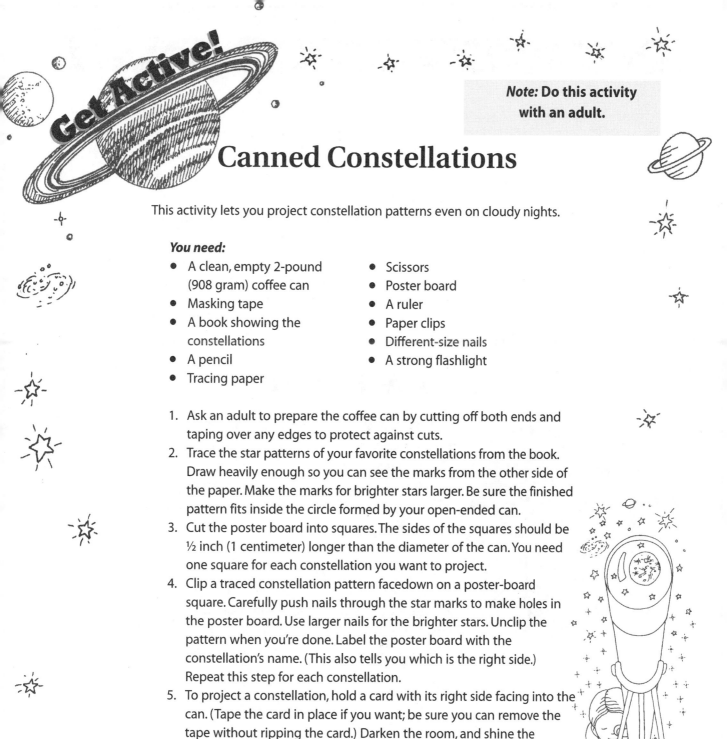

Get Active!

Canned Constellations

This activity lets you project constellation patterns even on cloudy nights.

You need:
- A clean, empty 2-pound (908 gram) coffee can
- Masking tape
- A book showing the constellations
- A pencil
- Tracing paper
- Scissors
- Poster board
- A ruler
- Paper clips
- Different-size nails
- A strong flashlight

1. Ask an adult to prepare the coffee can by cutting off both ends and taping over any edges to protect against cuts.
2. Trace the star patterns of your favorite constellations from the book. Draw heavily enough so you can see the marks from the other side of the paper. Make the marks for brighter stars larger. Be sure the finished pattern fits inside the circle formed by your open-ended can.
3. Cut the poster board into squares. The sides of the squares should be ½ inch (1 centimeter) longer than the diameter of the can. You need one square for each constellation you want to project.
4. Clip a traced constellation pattern facedown on a poster-board square. Carefully push nails through the star marks to make holes in the poster board. Use larger nails for the brighter stars. Unclip the pattern when you're done. Label the poster board with the constellation's name. (This also tells you which is the right side.) Repeat this step for each constellation.
5. To project a constellation, hold a card with its right side facing into the can. (Tape the card in place if you want; be sure you can remove the tape without ripping the card.) Darken the room, and shine the flashlight through the can's other end. Your constellation pattern will appear on the ceiling or wall.

dark matter. Scientists know it's there, however, because they can detect the effects of the matter's gravity.

The Sloan Digital Sky Survey in New Mexico suggests dark matter may make galaxies much larger than anyone thought. A typical galaxy's visible part has 100 billion stars and stretches 50,000 light-years. In 1999, the survey reported that dark matter may make galaxies span more than a million light-years into space. Their total mass could equal that of 5 trillion Suns.

If that's correct, the Milky Way and Andromeda Galaxies may be much closer neighbors than we thought. Indeed, the galaxies may almost brush up against each other!

A Star Is Born

How do stars like our Sun form? Gas molecules float few and far between in space. Because the distribution isn't even, gravity goes to work.

Gravity pulls some molecules closer to each other. Gas accumulates into huge clouds, called nebulas. These nebulas become star nurseries.

Some nebulas are visible with regular viewing telescopes. The Orion Nebula glows because it is heated by energy from other stars. The nebula in the Pleiades group of "seven sisters" stars reflects light from other stars. In other instances, dust blocks visible light. An example is the Horsehead Nebula, which just looks like a patch of dark sky.

Some gas forms rotating clusters. As more gas accumulates, the cluster spins faster—much the way skaters spin faster by pulling in their arms. At some point, the center of the cluster's core collapses. It's now a protostar, or newborn star.

The **protostar** is hidden from sight by gas and dust surrounding it. But scientists can detect protostars with telescopes

Galaxy Giggles

What is an astronomer's favorite candy?

Milky Ways™ and Mars™ Bars!

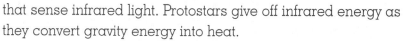

that sense infrared light. Protostars give off infrared energy as they convert gravity energy into heat.

The protostar is surrounded by a huge disk of material. Friction makes a lot of that material spiral inward toward the protostar. Planets can also form from material in this disk.

The protostar adds mass from the disk. Internal heat rises as it shrinks in size due to gravity. The young star also spins or "blows" some material off into space as it spins rapidly. Some such jets can stretch half a light-year away from the star.

Finally, internal temperatures exceed 10 million degrees Kelvin, or 18 million degrees Fahrenheit. Then the star starts nuclear fusion. In other words, it combines hydrogen atoms to form helium. The process gives off intense energy, which makes the star glow. The star has now entered the main part of its life.

There are, of course, variations. Often, twin stars are born as a binary star system. Binary stars rotate around their system's center of mass, called the Lagrange point.

WORDS to KNOW

protostar: a newly forming star. [PRO-toh-star]

Star Light, Star Bright

Astronomers measure stars' brightness with scales of magnitude. The smaller a star's apparent magnitude number is, the brighter it seems to us here on Earth.

Sirius, in the constellation Canis Major, is so bright that its apparent magnitude is −1.47 (less than zero). Vega, another bright star, has an apparent magnitude just over 0. Objects with an apparent magnitude over 6 can't be seen with the naked eye.

The Sun is obviously the brightest object in our sky. However, it's clearly not the biggest or most energetic star. If we were 33 light-years away, for instance, the Sun would seem as dim as the faintest star in the Little Dipper's handle.

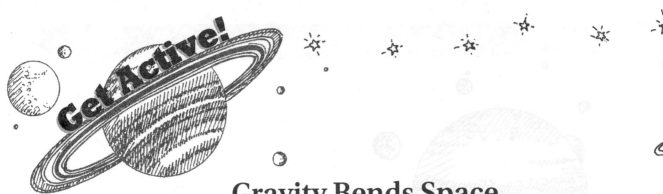

Gravity Bends Space

Gravity is the attraction objects have for each other. The more mass an object has, the stronger its gravitational pull is. See how gravity affects space.

You need:
- A yardstick
- A mattress covered with a sheet
- A tennis ball
- A clean bowling ball

1. Lay the yardstick on the mattress. Roll the tennis ball along the yardstick. It should travel in basically a straight line.
2. Place the bowling ball about a foot (30 centimeters) from the yardstick. Roll the tennis ball again, using the side of the stick closer to the bowling ball as a guide.
3. Did the tennis ball curve toward the bowling ball? Scientists have found similar distortions in space. Depending on how much bending occurs, the distortions can signal either a black hole or dark matter.

Luminosity measures how much energy a star emits. The most luminous stars tend to be the largest. For example, Rigel in the constellation Orion is a bright supergiant in Luminosity Class Ia. Polaris in Ursa Major is a "regular" supergiant star. Our Sun is in Luminosity Class V; it's an example of a main-sequence star.

Color also gives a clue about a star's heat and energy level. While stars look like twinkling white lights in the sky, there are also blue, red, and yellow stars.

Ask your parent to light a candle, and study the flame. Near the bottom, where fuel is burned, the flame looks blue. In the middle, the flame is yellow. The top edges, near the cooler air, appear reddish. In a similar way, a star's color tells how hot it is.

Astronomers use special instruments to study stars' light. Like a prism, the instruments show a spectrum, or rainbow band, of each star's light. Based on how the

Dark Matter

Use colored pencils or crayons to color the shapes using the color key, below. When you are finished, you will find what is hiding in this patch of empty-looking space.

0 = WHITE
1 = SILVER or LIGHT GREY
2 = BRIGHT BLUE
3 = BLACK

4 = RED
5 = PURPLE
6 = LIGHT BROWN

WORDS to KNOW

gravity: the attraction matter has for other matter. [GRAV-i-tee]

spectra look, astronomers classify stars into seven spectral classes: O, B, A, F, G, K, and M. Temperature wise, O stars are the hottest, with surface temperatures over 30,000°K. M stars are the coolest.

Generally, O and B stars are blue. A stars are white and F stars are yellow-white. G stars, like our Sun, are yellow. K stars are orange, and M stars are red.

Death of a Star

Stars use the hydrogen in their huge masses as fuel. Hydrogen is the lightest element, with one proton (positively charged particle) and one electron (negatively charged particle) in each atom. Through nuclear fusion, the star fuses hydrogen atoms into helium, which has two protons and two electrons. The process gives off immense amounts of energy.

Once the hydrogen is gone, the star is densely packed with helium atoms. And it wants to keep burning. So, **gravity**, pressure, and heat cause the star to start burning the helium.

Using nuclear fusion, it joins helium atoms to form heavier elements. The energy from these nuclear reactions extends the star's life. When the helium is gone, the star uses nuclear fusion to form still heavier elements. Thus, it forms atoms of oxygen, carbon, and other chemicals. The process continues all the way up to iron, which has 26 protons and electrons, plus various neutrons (atomic particles with no charge).

After producing iron, the star can't fuse any more elements to get energy. But other elements still form inside the old star. Neutrons can slip into atoms and become protons as negative charges get spit out to become electrons.

The star is dying, but all those heavier elements have now been formed. Some stars expand toward the end of their star lives. Then they shrink down into tiny "dwarfs." The dwarfs are

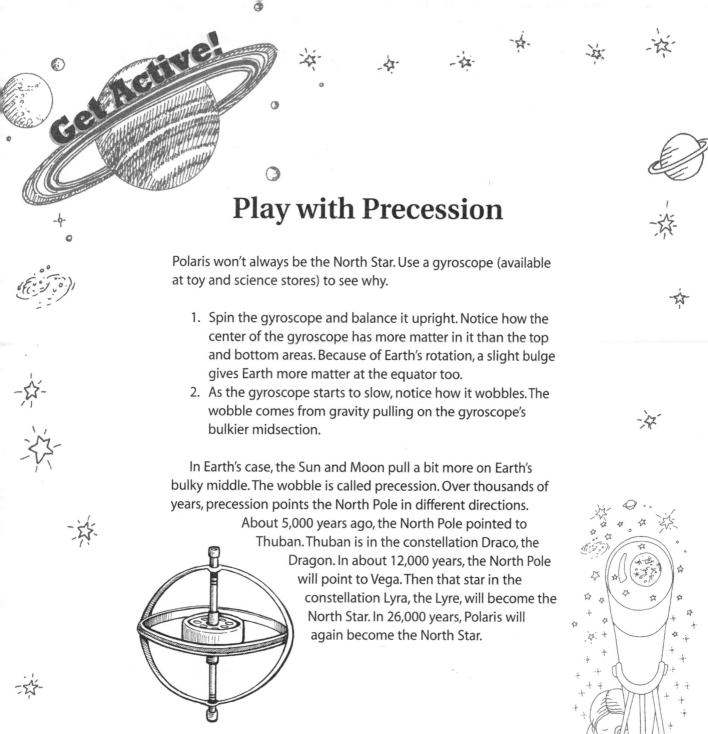

Play with Precession

Polaris won't always be the North Star. Use a gyroscope (available at toy and science stores) to see why.

1. Spin the gyroscope and balance it upright. Notice how the center of the gyroscope has more matter in it than the top and bottom areas. Because of Earth's rotation, a slight bulge gives Earth more matter at the equator too.
2. As the gyroscope starts to slow, notice how it wobbles. The wobble comes from gravity pulling on the gyroscope's bulkier midsection.

In Earth's case, the Sun and Moon pull a bit more on Earth's bulky middle. The wobble is called precession. Over thousands of years, precession points the North Pole in different directions. About 5,000 years ago, the North Pole pointed to Thuban. Thuban is in the constellation Draco, the Dragon. In about 12,000 years, the North Pole will point to Vega. Then that star in the constellation Lyra, the Lyre, will become the North Star. In 26,000 years, Polaris will again become the North Star.

WORDS to KNOW

nova: the sudden, thousandfold brightening of a star, toward the end of the star's life. A *supernova* is very similar, but involves a brightening of about a millionfold. [NOH-va]

neutron star: a small, densely packed star produced after certain novas; often called a *pulsar*. [NOO-tron star]

black hole: a collapsed mass whose gravity is so high that even light can't escape.

perhaps as big as Earth, yet their large mass gives them a strong gravity pull. This will likely be the fate of our Sun many millions of years from now.

Massive stars make a more spectacular exit. Once a red giant star's core holds too much iron, it starts to cool. When the cool core can no longer support the outer layers, the whole thing collapses. Then the collapsing gases suddenly bounce back in a huge explosion. Depending on its size, scientists call the explosion a **nova** or a supernova.

The huge explosion spreads large amounts of the heavier elements into space. These elements could find themselves pulled into gravity when yet another star forms. They might even wind up on planets like Earth.

Neutron Stars

What could be left after the explosion from a supernova? One answer is the **neutron star**. Compared to the former red giant, neutron stars are tiny—only about 9 miles (15 kilometers) across. That's only about the size of the city of Cleveland, Ohio.

Yet that tiny area holds as much matter as our Sun. A teaspoonful of material from a neutron star would weigh about three billion tons on Earth. That's heavy!

Because everything is squeezed so tightly, neutron stars are still extremely hot. Measurements range from 100,000 to 1,000,000 degrees Kelvin for some neutron stars.

Iron content within the neutron star produces a strong magnetic field. The neutron star is also spinning about 50 times per second, which produces electricity. The neutron star flings charged particles out into space along lines determined by its magnetic field.

Just as a lighthouse beam seems to flash as it spins, the neutron star's emissions seem to flash too. Scientists detect these "flashes" as radio wave pulses and sometimes as X-ray pulses. Thus, neutron stars are often called pulsars. The pulsing may continue for 10 million years or more.

Black Holes

Imagine a place where gravity is so strong that not even light can escape. That's what a **black hole** is.

These ghosts of giant stars have collapsed inward on themselves. Yet they have tremendous mass and an immense gravitational pull.

Black holes can't be seen with the naked eye. But scientists have proved their existence. For example, some stars seem to have matter pulled away from them. Scientists believe this is the pull of nearby black holes. Light energy also seems to "disappear" somewhere. Scientists say that somewhere would be a black hole.

Scientists now believe that gigantic black holes exist at the center of many galaxies. Among other things, their gravity would help hold the galaxies together.

A mass equal to 3 billion suns, for example, seems to sit at the center of a giant galaxy called M87 in the constellation Virgo. The Andromeda Galaxy also seems to have a central black hole that would weigh 30 million times the Sun's mass. Our own Milky Way may have a monstrous black hole at its center too.

Message from Deep Space

Imagine that you are on duty at a radio telescope when the first message comes in from an alien civilization! Follow the directions below to chart the radio pulses and decode the message.

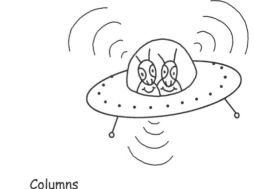

1. Column 1 and 5, all boxes — Grids 1, 10
2. Column 1 and 4, all boxes — Grid 3
3. Column 1, all boxes — Grids 2, 4, 5, 6, 7, 9, 11
4. Column 2, all boxes — Grid 8
5. Column 4, three middle boxes — Grid 11
6. Column 3, box 4 — Grids 4, 7
7. Column 4, boxes 2 and 5 — Grids 4, 7
8. Row 1, all boxes — Grids 8, 12
9. Row 5, all boxes — Grids 1, 2, 5, 8, 9, 12
10. Row 1 and 3, all boxes — Grids 2, 3, 5, 6, 9
11. Row 1 and 3, two middle boxes — Grids 4, 7
12. Row 1 and 5, two middle boxes — Grid 11
13. Row 3, box 4 — Grid 1
14. Box in very center of grid — Grid 1, 10, 12
15. Box to the upper left and lower right of the center box — Grid 10, 12

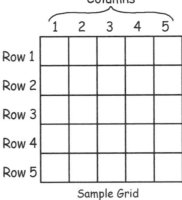

Columns

1 2 3 4 5

Row 1
Row 2
Row 3
Row 4
Row 5

Sample Grid

HINT:
Within each grid, boxes are numbered from left to right and top to bottom.

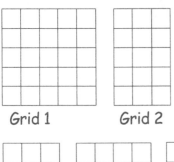

Grid 1   Grid 2   Grid 3   Grid 4   Grid 5

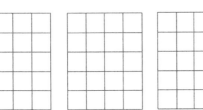
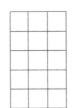
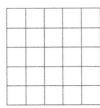
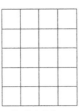
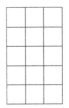

Grid 6   Grid 7   Grid 8   Grid 9   Grid 10   Grid 11   Grid 12

CHAPTER SEVEN
EXPLORING SPACE

The Space Race

On May 25, 1961, before a Special Joint Session of the United States Congress, President John Kennedy announced a new mission. He said, "I believe this nation should commit itself to achieving the goal, before the decade is out, of landing a man on the moon and returning him safely to Earth."

The United States had just launched its first astronaut into space on May 5, 1961. Alan Shepard's historic 15-minute flight took him 116 miles (186 kilometers) high above Earth. But Shepard was not the first human in space.

On April 12, 1961, the Soviet Union (now Russia and other countries) sent cosmonaut Yuri Gagarin into space aboard the *Vostok I* rocket. In 1957, the Soviet Union had also beaten the United States by launching *Sputnik I*. Circling Earth every 96 minutes, it was the first satellite in orbit.

Now the United States wanted to pull ahead in the space race. It was a matter of national security. The United States and the Soviet Union were not firing guns or bombs at each other. From the 1950s to the 1970s, however, the "cold war" kept them poised at the brink of war. If the Soviet Union conquered space and the Moon, then it could potentially win any attack against the United States.

Six single-person *Mercury* missions showed NASA could safely send astronauts into orbit. Next came two-person *Gemini* missions from 1964 through 1966. *Gemini* astronauts altered their spacecraft's orbit. They made the first space walks (called extravehicular activities, or EVAs). They used tools outside the spacecraft. *Gemini* spacecraft even docked with each other. People would have to know all these tasks for a Moon trip. Meanwhile, unmanned *Ranger* and *Surveyor* missions scouted out landing spots on the Moon.

Galaxy Giggles

Why would Jupiter be the best planet on which to own a car?

You'd never run out of gas!

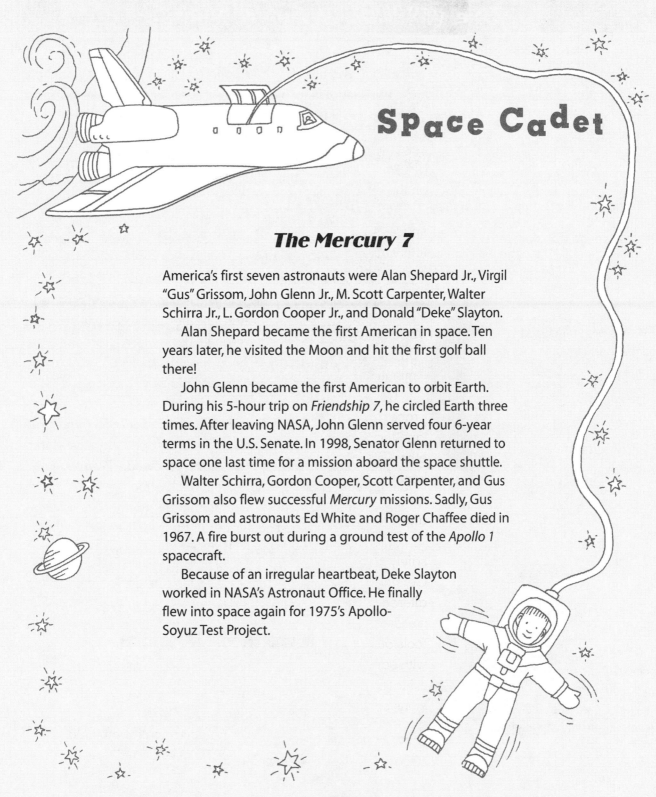

Space Cadet

The Mercury 7

America's first seven astronauts were Alan Shepard Jr., Virgil "Gus" Grissom, John Glenn Jr., M. Scott Carpenter, Walter Schirra Jr., L. Gordon Cooper Jr., and Donald "Deke" Slayton.

Alan Shepard became the first American in space. Ten years later, he visited the Moon and hit the first golf ball there!

John Glenn became the first American to orbit Earth. During his 5-hour trip on *Friendship 7*, he circled Earth three times. After leaving NASA, John Glenn served four 6-year terms in the U.S. Senate. In 1998, Senator Glenn returned to space one last time for a mission aboard the space shuttle.

Walter Schirra, Gordon Cooper, Scott Carpenter, and Gus Grissom also flew successful *Mercury* missions. Sadly, Gus Grissom and astronauts Ed White and Roger Chaffee died in 1967. A fire burst out during a ground test of the *Apollo 1* spacecraft.

Because of an irregular heartbeat, Deke Slayton worked in NASA's Astronaut Office. He finally flew into space again for 1975's Apollo-Soyuz Test Project.

Finally it was time for the Apollo program. *Apollo* spacecraft had three modules, or parts. Astronauts stayed mostly in the command module. The service module carried supplies and equipment. The lunar module would separate from the spacecraft to land on the Moon. Afterward, it would blast off and rendezvous with the command module. To escape Earth's gravity, the whole thing was loaded atop a powerful Saturn V rocket.

In 1968, *Apollo 8* became the first manned spacecraft to orbit the Moon. The photograph "Earthrise" showed humans what our world looks like from the Moon.

After two more flights, Americans were ready. On July 16, 1969, NASA launched *Apollo 11*. While Michael Collins piloted the command module, the lunar module landed on the Moon on July 20, 1969. "Houston. Tranquility Base here," radioed astronaut Neil Armstrong. "The Eagle has landed."

Several hours later, people around the world sat riveted to their televisions. A camera on the module's leg showed a white boot descending. "That's one small step for man, one giant leap for mankind," said Neil Armstrong as he stepped onto the Moon.

Minutes later, astronaut Buzz Aldrin followed. "Beautiful, beautiful," said Aldrin. "Magnificent desolation."

America had succeeded. Before the decade ended, it had sent people to the Moon and brought them home safely. A plaque left on the Moon says, "Here men from the planet Earth first set foot upon the Moon, July 1969 A.D. We came in peace for all mankind."

More Moon Missions

Apollo 13's crew nearly died after oxygen tanks exploded on April 13, 1970. To survive, astronauts James Lovell, Fred

Famous First Words

To solve this puzzle, figure out where to put each of the scrambled letters. They all fit in spaces under their own column. When you have correctly filled in the grid, you will have the answer to this question:

What were the first words that astronaut Neil Armstrong spoke as he stepped on to the surface of the moon?

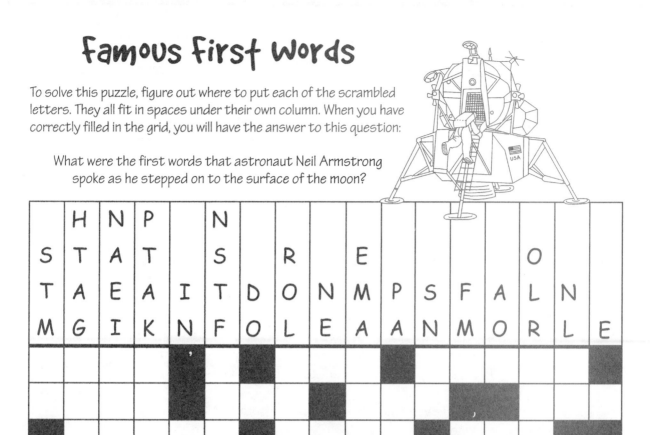

Haise, and Jack Swigert used the lunar module's life support. The lunar module wasn't made for three people, though. The astronauts could drink very little water and had to keep the cabin very cold.

Using the Moon's gravity field like a slingshot, *Apollo 13* aimed itself back to Earth. Then came a tricky re-entry into Earth's atmosphere. Despite all that went wrong, the astronauts landed safely.

Fortunately, America's other Moon missions went well. From 1969 to 1972, five more teams landed on the Moon. Astronauts drove around in a lunar rover, or "moon buggy." They collected rock samples. They did science experiments.

Get Active!

Note: Do this activity outside and away from windows and breakable objects. Ask an adult to help.

Blast Off

Rocket fuel propels, or pushes, spacecraft up and into space. Make your own miniature rocket.

You need:
- A pen
- A mailing label cut to fit film canister
- An empty 35-mm film canister (lid must fit inside the canister rim)
- An effervescent pain reliever tablet (such as Alka Seltzer®)
- Vinegar

1. Draw a rocket on the label. Stick it on the canister so the rocket's top points to the canister's bottom.
2. Break the tablet into four pieces. Set them aside.
3. Fill the canister two-thirds full with vinegar.
4. Do this step *very quickly*. Drop the tablet pieces in the canister and immediately snap the lid on. Promptly turn the canister upside down and set it on the ground. Move back 7 feet (2 meters).

Wait a minute or two. A chemical reaction between the vinegar and the tablet will make carbon dioxide gas build up inside your rocket. The gas will push the canister into the air.

How high did your rocket go? To get away from Earth's gravity, rockets need an escape velocity of 25,000 miles (40,000 kilometers) per hour. That equals 7 miles (11 kilometers) per second. That much speed requires huge, powerful rockets.

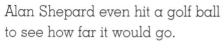

Alan Shepard even hit a golf ball to see how far it would go.

Then public interest in visiting the Moon waned. Moon missions were expensive, and policy makers felt the money could be better spent on Earth. They also wanted NASA to build reusable spacecraft to orbit Earth. Since 1972, no person has visited the Moon. Moon exploration resumed with the unmanned *Clementine* and *Lunar Prospector* missions in the 1990s.

Further Exploration

Unmanned missions throughout the solar system have brought us lots of knowledge. Here are some milestone missions.

Mariner 10—Mission to Mercury

In 1974, *Mariner 10* visited Mercury. In two fly-bys, it photographed one-third of the planet's cratered, Moon-like terrain.

Magellan Mission to Venus

Launched in May 1989, NASA's Magellan spacecraft spent four years orbiting Venus. Using radar, it mapped 98 percent of the planet's surface and collected lots of data about Venus.

Earlier Venus visits included *Mariner 2* in 1962, *Mariner 5* in 1967, and 1978's *Pioneer* Venus mission. The Soviet Union sent two *Vega* probes in 1985, plus various *Venera* missions from 1961 to 1983.

Mars Missions

The late 1990s began a 10-year series of Mars missions. NASA's *Mars Pathfinder* landed in 1997. It released Sojourner, a 2-foot (60-centimeter) long, six-wheeled, remote-control buggy. Running on solar batteries, Sojourner analyzed Mars's soil and sent back important new photos.

A later mission, the *Mars Global Surveyor*, also sent back important data. Although both the *Mars Climate Orbiter* and the *Mars Polar Lander* were lost in 1999, more missions are planned for the first decade of the 21st century.

NASA had earlier Mars missions too. From 1964 through 1972, *Mariner 4, 6, 7,* and *9* showed that Mars didn't have real canals or an advanced civilization. *Mariner 9* photo-mapped Mars's surface and studied its moons, Deimos and Phobos. The 1976 *Viking 1* and *2* missions sampled soil and made high-resolution images of Mars's entire surface. The Soviet Union also sent spacecraft to the red planet.

Galileo

After traveling for six years, NASA's *Galileo* spacecraft entered Jupiter's orbit in December 1995. Besides dropping a probe into the giant planet's atmosphere, *Galileo* has provided valuable information about Jupiter and its moons.

Cassini

Launched in 1999, *Cassini* will arrive at Saturn in 2004. It will also explore Phoebe, Titan, Dione, Rhea, Tethys, and some of Saturn's other moons. Of course, the spacecraft will

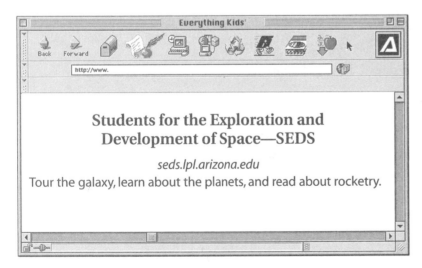

Students for the Exploration and Development of Space—SEDS

seds.lpl.arizona.edu
Tour the galaxy, learn about the planets, and read about rocketry.

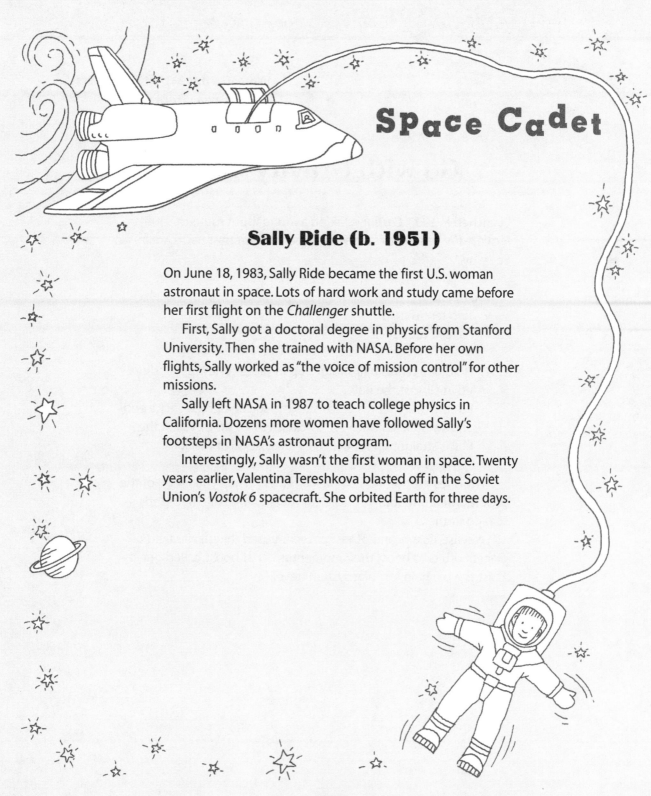

Space Cadet

Sally Ride (b. 1951)

On June 18, 1983, Sally Ride became the first U.S. woman astronaut in space. Lots of hard work and study came before her first flight on the *Challenger* shuttle.

First, Sally got a doctoral degree in physics from Stanford University. Then she trained with NASA. Before her own flights, Sally worked as "the voice of mission control" for other missions.

Sally left NASA in 1987 to teach college physics in California. Dozens more women have followed Sally's footsteps in NASA's astronaut program.

Interestingly, Sally wasn't the first woman in space. Twenty years earlier, Valentina Tereshkova blasted off in the Soviet Union's *Vostok 6* spacecraft. She orbited Earth for three days.

Go with Gravity Assist

Launched in 1997, *Cassini* is taking a roundabout route to Saturn. First *Cassini* headed toward Venus. Then it went past Earth again. See why.

You need:
- Two tennis balls
- A clean tube sock

1. Hold one tennis ball straight up in the air. Without winding up at all, toss the ball.
2. Put the other tennis ball inside the sock. Hold the sock's end, and swing it in large vertical circles three times. When the ball is straight up for the third time, let go of the sock.

Why does the second ball travel farther? When you let go of the sock, momentum from its "orbit" transfers to the ball. That sends it soaring farther.

Likewise, *Cassini* and other spacecraft used the gravity field of planets' orbits to boost their momentum. That boost, called gravity assist, is a big help for solar system travel.

zoom in on Saturn's spectacular rings.

Pioneer and Voyager

Pioneer 10 and 11 provided
close-up views of the outer
planets before continuing out
of our solar system. Pioneer
11, launched in 1973, sent its
last transmission in 1995.

Voyager 1 and 2 blasted off
in 1977. Voyager 1 visited
Jupiter and Saturn. Besides
those two planets, Voyager 2
visited Uranus in 1986 and
Neptune in 1989. It gave
people their first close-up
views of these blue giants.

Both Voyager spacecraft
are now outside the solar system and headed into deep space.
As this book goes to press, both Voyagers are still sending
data to NASA.

Astronomical Numbers

On to Taurus?

Launched in March 1972, Pioneer 10 is now more than 6.8
billion miles (10.9 billion kilometers) away. If nothing happens
to it, it will pass by one of the stars in the constellation Taurus,
the Bull, in about 2 million years.

A Fleet of Space Shuttles

All NASA spacecraft before 1980 were designed for one-time
use. The space shuttle, also called the Space Transportation
System, is a reusable space vehicle.

Measuring 184 feet (56 meters) long, the shuttle looks like a
space plane. It has engines, rocket boosters, a cargo bay, and
space for up to eight crew members. For takeoff, the shuttle

Robert Goddard (1882–1945)

As a boy, Robert Goddard loved H. G. Wells's story, *The War of the Worlds*. Could someone really build a rocket and escape Earth's gravity?

After studying civil engineering and physics, Robert became a rocket scientist. On March 16, 1926, he launched the first liquid-fuel rocket. It flew 184 feet (56 meters) high. Its speed peaked at 60 miles (100 kilometers) per hour.

Robert spent his career improving rockets. Although he died before any space missions were launched, Robert Goddard laid the foundation for modern space flight.

SPACE SHUTTLE EXPLORER

attaches to two rocket boosters. The boosters separate and fall into the ocean two minutes after blastoff.

Once in space, the shuttle "falls around" the Earth at about 1,800 miles (2,880 kilometers) per hour. Each orbit takes roughly 90 minutes. When its mission is complete, the shuttle brakes with its engines and re-enters the atmosphere. It glides to a landing on specially designed runways.

The first test shuttle was dubbed *Enterprise*, after the fictional *Star Trek* spaceship. Other shuttles that have flown include *Columbia*, *Atlantis*, *Challenger*, *Discovery*, and *Endeavor*. About 100 shuttle missions have occurred since 1981.

Sadly, disaster struck *Challenger's* tenth flight on January 28, 1986. Seventy-three seconds after blastoff, the shuttle exploded. All seven people aboard died: Francis Scobee, Michael Smith, Judith Resnik, Ellison Onizuka, Ronald McNair, Gregory Jarvis, and Christa McAuliffe. McAuliffe was a civilian schoolteacher who had planned to broadcast science lessons from space.

"The accident had a profound effect on everyone," recalls former astronaut Guy Bluford. Four of his close friends were on the flight.

After almost three years, the shuttle program resumed. Fortunately, no similar tragedy has occurred.

Toward International Cooperation

Slowly but surely, political tensions lessened between the United States and the former Soviet Union. In 1975, the two countries met each other halfway—while in orbit—for the Apollo-Soyuz Test Project. After learning each other's languages, an *Apollo* spacecraft docked in space with a Soviet

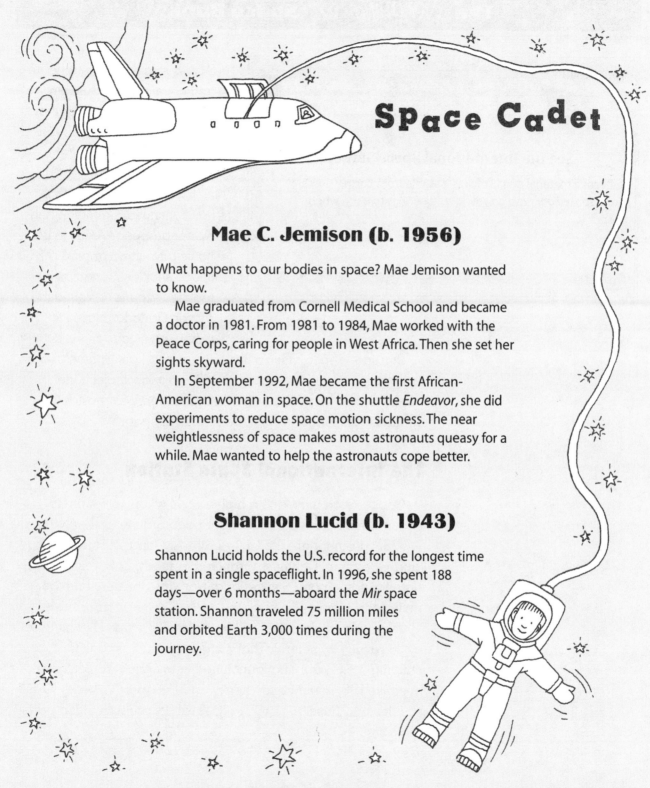

Space Cadet

Mae C. Jemison (b. 1956)

What happens to our bodies in space? Mae Jemison wanted to know.

Mae graduated from Cornell Medical School and became a doctor in 1981. From 1981 to 1984, Mae worked with the Peace Corps, caring for people in West Africa. Then she set her sights skyward.

In September 1992, Mae became the first African-American woman in space. On the shuttle *Endeavor*, she did experiments to reduce space motion sickness. The near weightlessness of space makes most astronauts queasy for a while. Mae wanted to help the astronauts cope better.

Shannon Lucid (b. 1943)

Shannon Lucid holds the U.S. record for the longest time spent in a single spaceflight. In 1996, she spent 188 days—over 6 months—aboard the *Mir* space station. Shannon traveled 75 million miles and orbited Earth 3,000 times during the journey.

See the International Space Station

Reflective material on ISS makes it visible from Earth. Go to *spaceflight.nasa.gov/realdata/sightings* to learn when to spot it.

Soyuz vessel. The astronauts and cosmonauts (Russian astronauts) worked together for several days. After separating, the spacecraft returned to Earth.

International cooperation has continued. Canadian and European Space Agency astronauts have flown aboard U.S. space shuttles. Canadian robotics experts designed the robotic Canadarm used to move large loads on the shuttle.

Starting in 1995, Russia invited American astronauts aboard its space station, *Mir*. Since the 1970s Skylab project, the United States hadn't had an orbiting station. *Mir* provided a chance to do longer-term experiments in space.

The International Space Station

Cooperation moved to a higher level when 16 countries began building the International Space Station (ISS) in 1999. The ISS partners are the United States, Canada, Russia, Brazil, Japan, Belgium, Denmark, France, Germany, Italy, the Netherlands, Spain, Switzerland, Norway, Sweden, and the United Kingdom.

When it's finished, ISS will measure 120 yards (110 meters) by 96 yards (88 meters). That's bigger than a football field. Building it on Earth and launching it into space wouldn't work because ISS would be too heavy and fall apart. Instead, NASA shuttles and Russian *Soyuz* spacecraft fly preassembled parts, called modules, into space. Astronauts then put the modules together as ISS orbits. Starting in 2000, three-person crews stayed aboard ISS to continue work between shuttle flights.

Putting everything together will take about 160 space walks and 46 assembly missions. If everything goes as planned, ISS should be finished by 2004. For 15 years after that, full crews of seven astronauts will take turns living and working aboard ISS.

Even after it's built, ISS will need regular supply visits. The crew will need air, water, food, and other items from Earth.

ISS is expensive. Its total cost is between $50 and $75 billion U.S. dollars. But the information gained from this huge floating science lab could be priceless.

Living in Space

Microgravity makes life in space a challenge. Microgravity is the weightlessness caused when a spacecraft is in free fall orbit (as with ISS or the shuttle) or when it escapes Earth's gravity (as in earlier Moon missions). Microgravity makes things float around in a spacecraft.

Thus, long, hot showers are out. All that water would float in

Dock to Dock

To dock, a space ship must fit a space station like a lock fits a key. Figure out where each of the six circling ships will fit. Then write each space ship's number on the correct docking port of the space station.

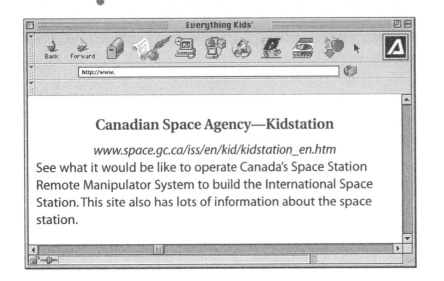

Canadian Space Agency—Kidstation

www.space.gc.ca/iss/en/kid/kidstation_en.htm
See what it would be like to operate Canada's Space Station Remote Manipulator System to build the International Space Station. This site also has lots of information about the space station.

the air! Astronauts usually take quick sponge baths instead.

On the space shuttle, crews choose their meals in advance. The meals are dehydrated (dried for storage) and packed in trays; astronauts then add water in flight. ISS will have freezers, so crews can have a broader selection of foods. But astronauts still can't get crumbs all over the place when they eat. And they need to pinch their drinking straws between sips to keep juice or coffee from floating out.

How do astronauts go to the bathroom? A plastic bag attaches to a seat to collect solid wastes. Toilet paper and wet wipes get sealed in the bag. Then the bag goes to a storage canister. It and other trash goes back to Earth for disposal. Urine goes into a wide vacuum hose and is sucked away. On the ISS, water from wastes can be recycled.

Astronauts strap themselves into bunks at bedtime. Otherwise, they'd float around all night.

Improving Life on Earth

Besides peering outward at the universe, space science focuses on planet Earth. In February 2000, for example, the shuttle *Endeavor* completed a massive mapping mission. Its data will help make better maps showing elevations and features on the ground.

Satellites help too. Weather satellites warn about upcoming storms. Satellites let telephones, computers, and televisions send information around the world.

Space also provides a unique opportunity for basic science research. We can't turn gravity off on the ground. But people and things falling around the Earth in a spacecraft are nearly weightless with respect to each other—a condition called microgravity.

Microgravity lets scientists experiment with how crystals grow, how proteins form, how fires burn, and lots of other concepts. People can use knowledge from those experiments to improve life on the ground. Eventually, they can make better medicines, improved electronics, stronger metals, and other products.

Beyond this, launching spacecraft and surviving in space takes lots of know-how. Temperatures can soar when sunlight shines on spacecraft or when friction heats them up as they re-enter Earth's atmosphere. But temperatures also drop far below freezing in the shade in the vacuum of space. Thus, anything sent into orbit needs to withstand both extreme hot and extreme cold.

Likewise, an emergency crew can't just drop by on a moment's notice if something goes wrong. Everything must work far away from the nearest electric power plant, fire hydrant, or repair shop. And, it must work in microgravity. Thus, throughout the space program, NASA engineers and contractors have had to develop new innovations and technologies. NASA's Office of Commercial Technology helps people put that knowledge to work on Earth. "We take technology that NASA engineers develop, and we try to apply it to the real world," explains Kathy Needham at the Glenn Research Center in Ohio.

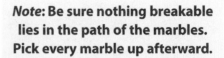

Falling in Orbit

Earth's gravity still pulls on orbiting spacecraft, like the space shuttle and the International Space Station. Fortunately, those spacecraft don't fall straight down. They fall *around* Earth.

You need:
- 3 marbles
- A flat table in a carpeted room

1. Push one marble slowly off the edge of the table. It should drop almost straight down.
2. Whack the second marble with your finger so it rolls off the table. The marble should fall in an arc.
3. Whack the third marble so it rolls really fast off the table. It should arc the farthest before landing.

What if your table were over 200 miles (322 kilometers) tall? And suppose you could whack the marble so it went 18,000 miles (29,000 kilometers) per hour. Then the marble's arc would match Earth's curve. It would be in free fall, like the International Space Station.

Things in free fall feel weightless. Because there's a tiny bit of attraction between things on a spacecraft, the term *microgravity* best describes the free fall state. Microgravity is also written as μg.

For the longest periods of microgravity, scientists need the free fall of Earth's orbit. For experiments lasting only a couple of seconds, NASA's Glenn Research Center in Ohio uses drop towers. Experiments are carefully set up and then dropped in free fall. Air bags at the bottom prevent major destruction.

For example, hospitals around the world use clear, flexible plastic tubing. The tubing is used for intravenous medicines, for donating blood, and for other purposes. NASA developed the tubing for its astronauts in the 1960s. The tubing collected urine when astronauts had to go in outer space.

Does your home have a smoke alarm? Have you ever used a rechargeable, cordless appliance? Both these innovations were originally developed for NASA's Apollo space program. Golf balls, vacuum cleaners, and home insulation are other examples of space age technology helping people here on Earth.

Doing Business in Space

Space has been "open for business" since 1962. That year, AT&T's *Telstar* became the first satellite to actively transmit communications. Today, hundreds of commercial satellites orbit the Earth. People rely on them for long-distance telephone service, computer connections, television broadcasts, and more.

What about actually doing business in space? In February, 2000, Russia agreed to let Amsterdam-based MirCorp use the space station *Mir*. Companies can pay MirCorp to do microgravity experiments in space.

NASA is exploring similar commercial opportunities. Future projects on board the shuttles or the International Space Station, for example, may be funded by private companies.

Antimatter and Wormholes

Antimatter particles have electrical charges that are opposite to those of regular matter. When matter and antimatter come in contact, they destroy each other. Theoretically, that should produce lots of energy.

Wormholes are also a theoretical possibility. These would be tunnel-like "shortcuts" through space.

SPACE SHUTTLE EXPLORER

Knowledge from the microgravity experiments would then let the companies develop better drugs, metals, or other products here on Earth.

A vacation in space, the "final frontier," may also lie in the future. Riding on a spacecraft or staying at a space station would be extremely expensive. But people may well pay for the thrill of space travel.

Other space entrepreneurs are springing up too. SpaceDev, for example, plans to send a spacecraft to a Near-Earth Asteroid. Clients would pay to put experiments on board.

Other ventures set their sites on the Moon. Again, tourism is a definite possibility, assuming lunar lodges were built. Meanwhile, why not virtually visit? Couldn't one take a look around and do sampling with a remote-controlled lunar rover? Working with Carnegie Mellon University's Robotics Institute, a company called LunaCorp is working to get this idea "off the ground." Another company, Applied Space Resources, hopes to bring surface samples back to Earth and sell them. Farther down the road, companies may even do mining and other activities on the Moon.

Who knows where the commercialization of space will lead? Quite literally, the sky's the limit.

Traveling Beyond the Solar System

Will we ever travel to other solar systems like science fiction characters? At present, spacecraft can go about 37,000 miles (59,000 kilometers) per hour. At those speeds, it would take 80,000 years to reach the nearest star. Clearly, that's not practical.

Build A Space Station

It takes a lot of cooperation and many pieces to put together a space station. To build the space station on this page, write the correct part number for each piece on the lines provided. The number shows where each piece belongs in the puzzle grid. We've given you a small picture of the completed station to guide you. Be careful! Because of the microgravity in space, some of the pieces may be floating upside-down!

Part ___

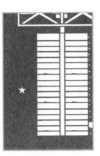

Part ___

Part ___

Part ___

Part ___

Part ___

Part ___

Part ___

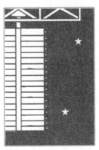

Part ___

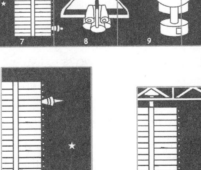

Part ___

Part ___

Part ___

Space Travelers

All kinds of things are moving around out in space. How many travelers can you track down and circle? Answers can go side to side, up and down, backwards and diagonally. When you are finished, read the leftover letters to see what is filling up the spaces between the words!

List of Space Travelers:

ALIEN
ASTEROID
BLACK HOLE
COMET
DUST
GALAXY
METEOR
MOON
NEBULA
PLANET

PROBE
PULSAR
RED GIANT
ROCKET
SATELLITE
SHUTTLE
SPACE JUNK
SPACE STATION
STAR
UFO

```
D  A  R  K  T  N  A  I  G  D  E  R
P  S  A  T  E  L  L  I  T  E  L  N
M  R  A  T  G  T  R  E  M  O  O  N
U  F  O  R  D  A  A  R  K  I  H  M
A  T  T  B  T  E  L  R  T  R  K  K
D  A  A  S  E  R  K  A  M  A  C  N
E  T  S  T  E  A  T  S  X  R  A  U
L  R  D  T  L  S  L  L  A  Y  L  J
T  R  O  I  E  K  D  U  S  T  B  E
T  M  E  C  A  R  T  P  B  T  E  C
U  N  A  R  K  R  O  E  T  E  M  A
H  P  L  A  N  E  T  I  D  A  N  P
S  R  C  O  M  E  T  K  D  M  A  S
```

NASA's Breakthrough Propulsion Physics team and other scientists are brainstorming about ways to travel near the speed of light or faster. Possible ideas include nuclear fusion, antimatter, and wormholes.

The challenge is figuring out how to get any of these ideas to work. But having the ideas means a crucial first step is already well underway. If people could get to the Moon in 10 years, who knows where people might travel in the next few centuries?

CHAPTER EIGHT
ARE WE ALONE?

The Roswell Incident

Has Earth been visited by creatures from outer space? On June 14, 1947, William Brazel and his eight-year-old son Vernon were making rounds on a New Mexico ranch. Scattered over a large area, they found an assortment of rubble that resembled rubber strips, sticks, tinfoil, and tough paper. The nearby Air Force base sometimes flew weather balloons. But this debris didn't look like it came from an ordinary weather balloon.

About 10 days later, someone in Washington State claimed he saw "flying saucers." The more Brazel thought about it, the more he believed the debris he found might come from a flying saucer too. On July 7, 1947, he reported his find to the sheriff in Roswell, New Mexico.

Officers from the Roswell Army Air Field collected the debris and took it back to their base. Immediately the *Roswell Daily Record* published the headline "RAAF Captures Flying Saucer on Ranch in Roswell Region."

The Air Force denied rumors of a flying saucer. It said the debris was part of a radar reflector from a new kind of weather balloon. "Flying Disc Explained," reported the newspapers.

Roswell received little attention for about 30 years. Then a *National Enquirer* story and a book called *The Roswell Incident* revived the story. Based on new recollections, the book claimed that an alien spacecraft had indeed crashed, shortly after being hit by lightning. It said the military removed alien bodies from the crash site and covered up the truth.

Similar reports continued through the 1990s. One 1995 television special even claimed to show footage of an alien autopsy. The film's owners, however, refused to let experts examine it to see if the film really was made in 1947.

To date, no one has proved that the Roswell incident involved aliens from outer space. But the story continues to spur other reports about UFOs (unidentified flying objects).

UFOs in Tabloids and Talk Shows

Most reports of UFO sightings and alien encounters are unreliable. Many are told only in newspapers sold at supermarket checkout counters. Others are reported only on talk shows that specialize in bizarre, sensational topics. When the media reporting alleged alien encounters lack a solid reputation, the reports can't be believed.

Indeed, many UFO stories are made up so people can get attention through such media. Other stories come from people who lack a firm grip on reality.

UFO sightings by rational people often turn out to have reasonable explanations. Careful examination usually shows that the people were honestly mistaken about storms or other natural events. A few reports remain unexplained. However, those reports also provide no reliable evidence that the event was an alien visit from space.

The presence of alien life is so important that scientists want positive proof. In other words, someone claiming that aliens have visited should prove it actually happened. They cannot simply say, "What else can it be?"

Indeed, if intelligent creatures visited us from another world, it would be a great event. Friendly aliens would probably announce their presence. Such "first contact" would open avenues for both cultures to learn about each other. If alien visitors were unfriendly, we'd probably

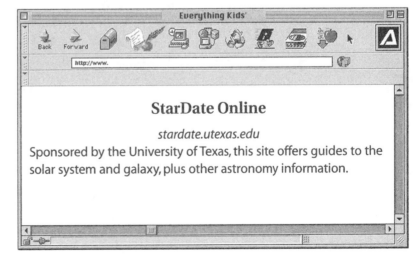

StarDate Online

stardate.utexas.edu

Sponsored by the University of Texas, this site offers guides to the solar system and galaxy, plus other astronomy information.

Ancient Mysteries

Giant stone figures sit on Easter Island in the Pacific Ocean. Who built the figures and why is a mystery.

Some people think the Easter Island figures were built by creatures from another planet. Primitive cultures, they claim, could not have made such marvels.

Such arguments have surface appeal. However, they're just another case of "what else can it be" reasoning. We can't assume all our ancestors were dummies. After all, they survived without electricity, telephones, television, computers, and fast food.

SPACE SHUTTLE EXPLORER

know about that too. After all, people tend to notice when someone attacks.

Have aliens visited us from space? So far, there's no reliable evidence that they have. But that doesn't mean that alien creatures aren't out there, somewhere, in space.

Recipe for Alien Life

If life exists elsewhere in the universe, it needs several things. First, it needs somewhere to live. That calls for a planet or moon.

Liquid water is also required for life as we know it. Water provides a way for chemicals to get together with each other and react. Those reactions make it possible for complex molecules to form.

The building blocks for those molecules would also be needed. Life on Earth, for example, is carbon based. The molecules of our bodies' cells have carbon in them, as do other life forms on our planet. Thus, "life as we know it" probably requires organic compounds with carbon in them. Some scientists speculate that silicon life forms might also be possible.

Even having all these things doesn't guarantee that life will be present. A planet or moon may be too hot or cold. Its gravity may be too strong. Its atmosphere may be poisonous. Or other factors could preclude life.

Even if life exists, it may not be life "as we know it." Single-celled organisms have been found under Antarctica's ice, deep in the ocean, and even deep underground. But that doesn't mean we can interact with those life forms in the meaningful manner fancied by science fiction writers.

Despite all this, some scientists say there may well be thousands of civilizations out in space. In 1961, astronomer Frank Drake suggested a mathematical approach to the question.

His approach would multiply the number of Sun-like stars born each year in the Milky Way by the fraction of those stars with planets. The result would be multiplied again by the fraction of planets that were like Earth, the fraction of those planets that actually developed life, and the fraction of planets where that life would be intelligent. The result would be multiplied further by the fraction of planets where intelligent creatures would develop technology within the number of years that their civilization would exist. The result would be only a tiny fraction of the original number of Sun-like stars.

Of course, no one knows what numbers would be plugged into the equation. Thus, no one can realistically say how many intelligent civilizations might exist in the Milky Way or any other galaxy. Drake's own guess was 10,000.

Other scientists, like Donald Brownlee at the University of Washington, think such estimates are too optimistic. The Sun may not be a "typical" star, and Earth may be a very unusual planet. Our orbit is just the right distance from the Sun. The planet's climate is relatively stable. There's enough carbon for life, but not so much that we have a torrid greenhouse atmosphere like Venus.

Beyond this, Earth has survived 65 million years without a major extinction from a comet or asteroid. Our planet's geology also produces different types of environments. That helped give humans and other species a better chance to thrive.

Given the vastness of space, searching for another civilization may well be like looking for a needle in a haystack. Even if we could find one, it may be too far away for any back-and-forth communication.

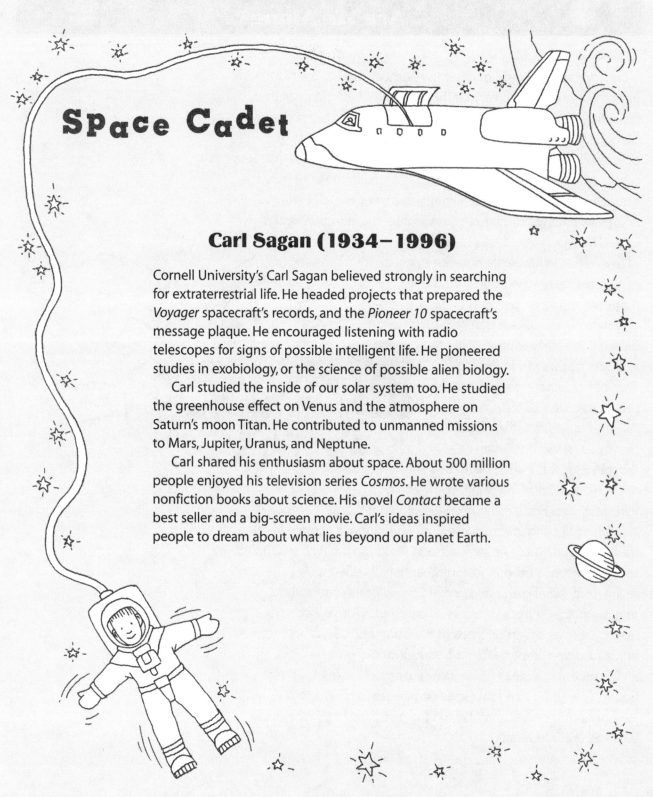

Space Cadet

Carl Sagan (1934–1996)

Cornell University's Carl Sagan believed strongly in searching for extraterrestrial life. He headed projects that prepared the *Voyager* spacecraft's records, and the *Pioneer 10* spacecraft's message plaque. He encouraged listening with radio telescopes for signs of possible intelligent life. He pioneered studies in exobiology, or the science of possible alien biology.

Carl studied the inside of our solar system too. He studied the greenhouse effect on Venus and the atmosphere on Saturn's moon Titan. He contributed to unmanned missions to Mars, Jupiter, Uranus, and Neptune.

Carl shared his enthusiasm about space. About 500 million people enjoyed his television series *Cosmos*. He wrote various nonfiction books about science. His novel *Contact* became a best seller and a big-screen movie. Carl's ideas inspired people to dream about what lies beyond our planet Earth.

As a result, some people think the search for extraterrestrial life is too great a long shot to justify the time and money that would be required. Despite the odds, other people are definitely looking.

Prospecting for Planets

A planet or moon is the first requirement for possible life beyond Earth. In 1995, scientists discovered the first planet outside our solar system. What they've discovered so far is nothing at all like Earth.

Planets are nowhere near as large as the stars they orbit. They also don't radiate light the way stars do. Thus, the first planets discovered couldn't be seen directly. Instead, scientists analyzed data over time from different parts of the sky. They looked for a wobble, similar to the tug that a puppy might give while running around on a leash. The wobble pulls the star either closer to or farther from Earth. That movement shows up as a tiny Doppler shift in the star's light. The light is a little bluer as objects move closer, and a bit more red as they move farther away.

After years of study, Swiss astronomers Michel Mayor and Didier Queloz found a planet orbiting the star 51 Pegasi. American scientists Geoff Marcy and Paul Butler confirmed their findings. Using similar methods, they and other scientists have now discovered about 30 planets outside our solar system.

Indeed, Upsilon Andromedae, in the constellation Andromeda, apparently has three planets orbiting it. That qualifies as a regular solar system!

The discoveries raise lots of questions. The planet orbiting 51 Pegasi, for example, is huge. It's about as large as Jupiter. Also, its orbit is far closer to the star than Jupiter is in our solar system. Gas giants have also been found orbiting close to other stars.

Galaxy Giggles

Which one of Santa's reindeers do astronomers like best?

Comet!

125

"Keep On Looking"

The universe isn't just big—it's huge, gigantic, immense, VAST! Looking for other life forms in outer space is like looking for a...well, how about looking for the one small letter "i" in this book that has two dots over the top instead of one? Look on every page, in all the corners and in all the pictures, too. Maybe it's in the Table of Contents or the Glossary. It could be ANYwhere. If you find it, congratulations—you have made first contact!

Scientists had previously thought that gas giants only formed near the cooler, outer edges of the disks circling newly formed stars.

In 1999, British astronomers reported the first actual view of an extrasolar planet. They focused their study around the star [τ] Boötis (for Tau Boötis). The star is "just" 50 light-years away, and a planet was detected near it in 1997.

Because the planet was very close to the star, it glowed with reflected light. Yet the star shines more than 10,000 times brighter. To see the planet, the scientists had to filter the star's light carefully.

Based on their studies, the scientists announced that the planet was even bigger than Jupiter, with about eight times its mass. They also announced that the planet had a bluish-green color. Other teams of scientists are working to confirm the results and to discover more planets.

The Jupiter-like giant planets found so far could not support life as we know it. Because they're so close to stars, they would be too hot. They could also have crushing gravity and no solid surface. However, these are just the first planets scientists are finding beyond our solar system. Who knows what they may find in the future?

"Letters in a Bottle"

How do you get in touch with someone far away? On Earth, you can call on the phone. You can mail a letter. You can send e-mail. These techniques don't work well for communicating with other solar systems. But Earth has already sent messages out into the universe anyway.

The *Pioneer 10* and *11* spacecraft carried small metal plaques. The plaques identified the origin of the spacecraft. That way, any alien species who found them would know where and when they came from.

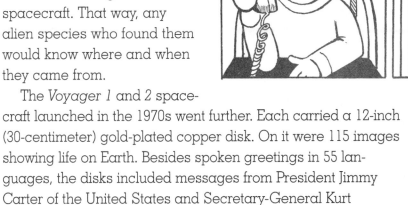

The *Voyager 1* and 2 spacecraft launched in the 1970s went further. Each carried a 12-inch (30-centimeter) gold-plated copper disk. On it were 115 images showing life on Earth. Besides spoken greetings in 55 languages, the disks included messages from President Jimmy Carter of the United States and Secretary-General Kurt Waldheim of the United Nations.

The record's soundtrack also included natural sounds like surf, wind, and animals, plus musical selections from different cultures. Among its 90-minutes of music was the Rolling Stones' song, "I Can't Get No Satisfaction." Of course, each *Voyager* spacecraft also included instructions on how to play the record.

Since 1990, both spacecraft have been traveling beyond the solar system. Neither will get close to any other planets for 40,000 years. The chances that an alien civilization will find the records seems remote. "The spacecraft will be encountered and the record played only if there are advanced spacefaring civilizations in interstellar space," noted Carl Sagan, who chaired the committee that designed the record. "But the

launching of this bottle into the cosmic ocean says something very hopeful about life on this planet."

A different form of message is radio signals. Puerto Rico's Arecibo radio telescope opened in 1974. Scientists aimed a transmitter at the M13 globular cluster of stars. The cluster is 26,000 light-years from Earth. Optimistically, they sent a series of 1,679 radio signal pulses.

The pulses can be arranged in an even grid in only two ways. One arrangement is meaningless. But when anyone tries the other way—73 rows of 23 pulses—they'll get picture information about Earth. The picture shows a human figure and tells its height. It gives Earth's population and tells about our bodies' chemistry. It tells where Earth is in our solar system.

We are constantly sending other signals too. Television and radio signals are routinely beamed into space. Some bounce back via telecommunications satellites. Others keep traveling off into space. Perhaps some civilization within 50 light-years has already detected those signals. What might they think about our news programs, music, dramas, and situation comedies?

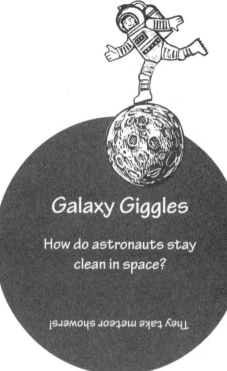

Galaxy Giggles

How do astronauts stay clean in space?

They take meteor showers!

Listening for Aliens: The SETI Search

We've tried contacting creatures from other planets. Perhaps they've already tried to send radio signal messages to us. SETI, the Search for Extraterrestrial Intelligence, thinks that just may be possible. Based in California, the organization's members "listen" to radio signals from space. Since the 1960s, various projects have scanned the sky for signs of extraterrestrial life.

SETI researchers don't just sit around with headphones. Rather, they use computers to analyze signals picked up from

What Would You Say?

How would you design your own Arecibo-type message to an alien world? If your message were beamed as a signal, it would be sent in binary code as a series of "on" and "off" pulses. Instead of Base 10 (the regular numbers we use), binary code uses Base 2 (1, 10, 11, 100, etc.), combinations of 1 and 0. Prepare your message in a grid. Each shaded square would represent a 1. Each unshaded square would represent a 0.

You need:
- A ruler
- A pencil
- Graph paper
- Tape
- Scissors
- Paper towel tube

1. Decide on your grid's dimensions. You want your message to be easy to decode. Thus, you should pick prime numbers. Prime numbers can only be divided by themselves and 1. Prime numbers would give aliens only two ways of arranging the numbers in an even grid. One of those will be your picture!
2. Use the ruler and pencil to outline your grid. Count carefully. Tape sheets of graph paper together on the back if you need more space.
3. After you prepare the grid, darken squares to "code" your message. You may want to include a human figure or a diagram of the solar system. You may want to show your house or a pet.
4. When you've finished, cut out your grid. Label the back with your name and date. Then roll it up and store it in a paper towel tube. Look at the message again in several weeks. What would you think about the message if you were an alien?
5. For more of a challenge, write out your message as a series of 1s (for shaded squares) and 0s (for blank squares). Then exchange messages with a friend. Can you decode each other's message to reproduce its pictures on graph paper?

SETI: The Search for Extraterrestrial Intelligence

www.seti.org
Learn about efforts to find extraterrestrial intelligence in the universe. With your parents' permission and the right computer equipment, you can even help at home.

space. Most signals are just background "noise" from bodies in the galaxy. Thus, the computers scan for signs that a signal is intentional and meaningful, rather than just random.

Do you want to help search for extraterrestrials? Since 1999, the SETI@home program has let people download free software for their home computers. The software seems to run like a screen saver. Screen savers are programs that produce moving images when someone isn't doing other work on the computer. The programs make computer screens last longer by preventing a single image from being "burned" onto the screen.

Unlike ordinary screen savers, SETI@home is really at work. The program gets data from the huge Arecibo radio telescope in Puerto Rico. It analyzes the data for possible signs of extraterrestrial intelligence. The program sends its analysis to SETI. Then it downloads another chunk of data to study.

During the first nine months of SETI@home, about 1.6 million people in over 200 countries downloaded software. In that time, SETI estimates that volunteers donated the equivalent of 165,000 years of computing time to the search for alien life. Sun Microsystems and Intel Performance Labs both donated over 100 years of computer time. A. W. Spence Middle School in Dallas was also a generous volunteer, with 25 years of computer time logged for the program.

You can learn more at *setiathome.ssl.berkeley.edu*. As always, be sure to get your parents' okay before downloading *anything* from the Internet to a home computer.

Glossary

asteroid: a small, rocky world that orbits the Sun. [AS-tur-oyd]

astronomy: the study of space. [a-STRON-uh-mee]

black hole: a collapsed mass whose gravity is so high that even light can't escape.

comet: a "dirty snowball" of ice that orbits the Sun and produces tails of gas and dust when it's near the Sun. [COM-et]

crater: round indentation made by the impact of an object from space on a planet or moon. [CRAY-tur]

eclipse: the blocking of light from one object in space by another. In a *solar eclipse*, the Moon keeps all or part of the Sun's light from reaching parts of Earth. In a *lunar eclipse*, Earth blocks the Sun's light from reaching the Moon. [ee-CLIPS]

ellipse: a closed curve whose every point is the sum of the distances from two points, called *foci*; an oval. [ee-LIPS]

galaxy: a huge group of stars, gas, dust, and other matter orbiting their common center of mass. [GAL-ax-ee]

gravity: the attraction matter has for other matter. [GRAV-i-tee]

light-year: the distance light travels in one year; about 5.9 trillion miles or 9.4 trillion kilometers.

matter: the "stuff" that makes up the physical universe; generally, anything that has weight and takes up space.

meteor: a body of matter from space that's heated by friction and glows as it falls through Earth's atmosphere. The body is a *meteoroid* before it enters Earth's atmosphere. Anything that survives to land on the ground is called a *meteorite*. [MEE-tee-or]

moon: a body in space that orbits a planet.

neutron star: a small, densely packed star produced after certain novas; often called a *pulsar*. [NOO-tron star]

nova: the sudden, thousandfold brightening of a star, toward the end of the star's life. A *supernova* is very similar, but involves a brightening of about a millionfold. [NOH-va]

nuclear fusion: the process by which stars produce tremendous amounts of energy by joining atoms of one element to form another element. [NOO-clee-ar FYOO-shun]

orbit: travel around another body in space in a regular path. [OR-bit]

planet: a spherical, nonshining body that orbits a star. Planets generally are larger than asteroids, although a few asteroids are larger than Pluto. [PLAN-et]

protostar: a newly forming star. [PRO-toh-star]

rotate: to spin on an axis. [RO-tate]

solar system: the Sun and its associated planets, asteroids, comets, and so on. [SO-lur SIS-tem]

star: a shining globe of gas that makes energy by nuclear fusion.

Resources

Organizations

National Aeronautics and Space Administration
NASA Headquarters
Washington, D.C. 20546
NASA's headquarters are in Washington, D.C.
Research centers are located throughout the United
States.
www.spaceflight.nasa.gov

Canadian Space Agency
6767 route de l'Aeroport
Saint-Hubert, Quebec J3Y 8Y9 Canada
www.space.gc.ca

SETI Institute
2035 Landings Drive
Mountain View, CA 94043
www.seti.org

Magazines

The following magazines frequently feature articles and information about astronomy and space exploration:

Astronomy
Discover
Odyssey
Sky & Telescope
YES Mag

Books

Beatty, J. Kelly, Carolyn Collins Petersen, and Andrew Chaikin, eds. *The New Solar System.* 4th ed. Cambridge, Mass.: Sky Publishing Corp., 1999.

Bond, Peter. *DK Guide to Space: A Photographic Journey Through the Universe.* New York: DK Publishing, Inc., 1999.

Briggs, Carole S. *Women in Space.* Rev. ed. Minneapolis, Minn.: Lerner Publications Company, 1999.

Dyson, Marianne J. *Space Station Science: Life in Free Fall.* New York: Scholastic Inc., 1999.

Engelbert, Phillis, and Diane L. Dupuis. *The Handy Space Answer Book.* Detroit, Mich.: Visible Ink, 1998.

Fradin, Dennis. *The Planet Hunters: The Search for Other Worlds.* New York: Margaret K. McElderry Books, 1997.

Kaufmann, William J., and Roger A. Freedman. *Universe.* 5th ed. New York: W. H. Freeman & Co., 1999.

Kurland, Michael. *The Complete Idiot's Guide to Extraterrestrial Intelligence.* New York: Alpha Books, 1999.

Miller, Ron. *The History of Rockets.* New York: Franklin Watts, 1999.

Moore, Patrick. *The Observer's Year: 366 Nights of the Universe.* London: Springer Verlag, 1998.

North, Gerald. *Astronomy Explained.* London: Springer Verlag, 1997.

Scott, Elaine. *Close Encounters: Exploring the Universe with the Hubble Space Telescope.* New York: Hyperion Books for Children, 1998.

Seeds, Michael A. *Horizons: Exploring the Universe.* 6th ed. Pacific Grove, Calif.: Brooks/Cole, 2000.

Shirley, Donna, with Danielle Morton. *Managing Martians.* New York: Broadway Books, 1998.

Time-Life Editors. *Space & Planets.* Alexandria, Va.: Time-Life Books, 1992.

VanCleave, Janice. *Janice VanCleave's Constellations for Every Kid.* New York: John Wiley & Sons, 1997.

Wills, Steve. *Mind-Boggling Astronomy.* Peterborough, N.H.: Cobblestone Publishing, 1995.

Answers

page 10 • **Take a Closer Look**

1. N9 2. I 10 3. F7 4. D3 5. D9 6. L9 7. C4 8. J2

page 17 • **Leaving Home**

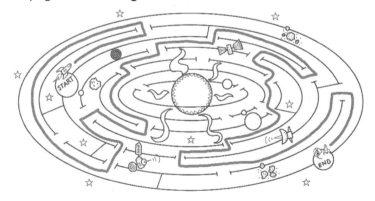

page 21 • **Solar Poetry**

Twinkle, twinkle, little __STAR__,

I used to wonder what you __ARE__.

   (Now I know EVERYTHING!)

When hydrogen meets __HYDROGEN__

And fuse to create __HELIUM__,

You, in the process, shine so __BRIGHT__

You twinkle, twinkle, day and __NIGHT__

page 29 • **Making Faces**

Write the letters of the secret name in the boxes provided.

| T | H | E | | M | A | N | | I | N |

| T | H | E | | M | O | O | N |

Answers

page 44 • Pathfinder

page 45 • Good Night!

1. Print the words "moon and stars" leaving out the spaces between the words.	MOONANDSTARS
2. Move the 4th letter to the 1st position.	NMOOANDSTARS
3. Delete the letter R.	NMOOANDSTAS
4. Change the D to an L.	NMOOANLSTAS
5. Replace the 2nd and 8th letters with the letter I.	NIOOANLITAS
6. Replace both letters A with the letter G.	NIOOGNLITGS
7. Change both letters O to the letter H.	NIHHGNLITGS
8. Switch the 9th and the 10th letters with each other.	NIHHGNLIGTS
9. Switch the 4th and the 5th letters with each other.	NIHGHNLIGHS
10. Change the middle letter to the letter T.	NIHGHTLIGHS
11. Move the middle letter between the last two letters.	NIHGHLIGHTS
12. Change the 3rd letter to the letter T.	NITGHLIGHTS
13. Take the 3rd letter and move it between the H and the L.	NIGHTLIGHTS

page 50 • Mars Colony Groupie

1. TCSAEUIPSS — SPACESUITS
2. ENACIMHS — MACHINES
3. DOFO — FOOD
4. SLAPNT — PLANTS
5. YXEOGN — OXYGEN
6. EAETRHS — HEATERS
7. ERVSRO — ROVERS
8. DEMO — DOME
9. EAWRT — WATER

page 65 • Can You Get There From Here?

Go from HERE to THERE in one step.

1. Add a T to the beginning of the word!

Go from SHUTTLE to HUBBLE in two steps.

1. Delete the letter S (HUTTLE)

2. Change the letters T to B (HUBBLE)

Go from EARTH to MARS in three steps.

1. Change the E to an M (MARTH)

2. Change the T to an S (MARSH)

3. Delete the letter H (MARS)

Go from URANUS to SATURN in four steps.

1. Reverse the whole word (SUNARU)

2. Switch the 2nd and 4th letters (SANURU)

3. Change the N to a T (SATURU)

4. Change the last letter to an N (SATURN)

Answers

page 78 • Meteor Missiles

page 96 • Message from Deep Space

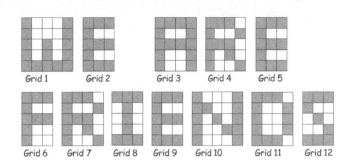

Grid 1   Grid 2   Grid 3   Grid 4   Grid 5

Grid 6   Grid 7   Grid 8   Grid 9   Grid 10   Grid 11   Grid 12

page 83 • Pictures in the Stars

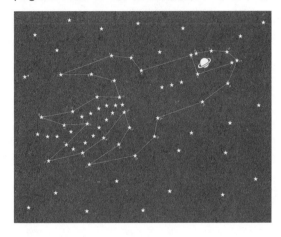

page 101 • Famous First Words

	H	N	P		N										
S	T	A	T		S		R		E					O	
T	A	E	A	I	T	D	O	N	M	P	S	F	A	L	N
M	G	I	K	N	F	O	L	E	A	A	N	M	O	R	L	E
T	H	A	T	'	S		O	N	E		S	M	A	L	L	
S	T	E	P		F	O	R		M	A	N		,		O	N	E
	G	I	A	N	T		L	E	A	P		F	O	R	
M	A	N	K	I	N	D									

page 91 • Dark Matter

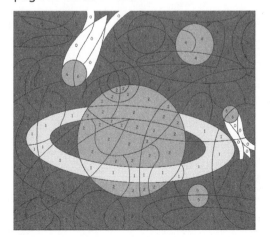

135

Answers

page 111 • **Dock to Dock**

page 118 • **Space Travelers**

page 117 • **Build a Space Station**

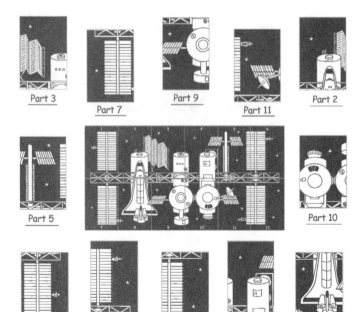

Part 3

Part 7

Part 9

Part 11

Part 2

Part 5

Part 10

Part 1

Part 6

Part 12

Part 4

Part 8

page 126 • **"Keep Looking"**

The "ï" can be found on page 33 (Eclïpses).

EVERYTHING®

Trade paperback, $9.95
1-58062-322-0, 144 pages

The Everything® Kids' Money Book
by Diane Mayr

From allowances to money gifts, from lemonade stands to lawn-mowing businesses, *The Everything® Kids' Money Book* tells kids how to make money, save money, and spend money. It also has fascinating information about currency, an introduction to the stock market, and even some fun money-based games. Basically, this book is filled with everything a kid would want to know about money.

The Everything® Kids' Puzzle Book
by Jennifer A. Ericsson & Beth L. Blair

Stuck inside on a rainy day? Trapped in a car for a long trip? Just love puzzles? This is your book! From crosswords to mazes to picture puzzles, this book is filled with hours of puzzling fun. As an added bonus, every space that doesn't have a puzzle in it is filled with fascinating facts and funny jokes. You'll never be bored with *The Everything® Kids' Puzzle Book* by your side!

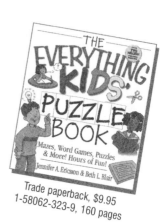

Trade paperback, $9.95
1-58062-323-9, 160 pages

See the entire Everything® series at www.adamsmedia.com/everything